Heather Butler has taught at primary level for over 25 years with a particular emphasis on special needs. Since becoming RE subject leader six years ago, she has worked on ideas and resources to help children learn from *RE as much as* about *RE, believing that the application of learning is the key to a good RE lesson* and *spirituality* ll as *whole-school stor* d INSET

Heather is also in w th a charity training ad who work with traumati d children in Croatia, lead iting workshops at the Roald Dahl Museum and Story Centre in Buckinghamshire and is a mentor for the National Association of Writers in Education. She is the author of many books, including plays, assembly material, short stories and resource books for teachers.

35 Stories to Make You Think *reworks the material in her three books published by* Barnabas, Stories to Make You Think, More Stories to Make You Think *and* Further Stories to Make You Think.

Heather's website can be found at www.heatherbutler.info and she can be contacted for INSET training or workshops in schools at thesiding@btinternet.com.

G000139983

Text copyright © Heather Butler 2008
Illustrations copyright © Simon Smith 2008
The author asserts the moral right
to be identified as the author of this work

Published by
The Bible Reading Fellowship
15 The Chambers, Vineyard
Abingdon OX14 3FE
United Kingdom
Tel: +44 (0)1865 319700
Email: enquiries@brf.org.uk
Website: www.brf.org.uk

Stories to Make You Think published 1999
More Stories to Make You Think published 2001
Further Stories to Make You Think published 2004
This compilation first published 2008

ISBN 978 1 84101 506 4
10 9 8 7 6 5 4 3 2 1 0
All rights reserved

Acknowledgments
Unless otherwise stated, scripture quotations are taken from the Contemporary
English Version of the Bible published by HarperCollins Publishers, copyright
© 1991, 1992, 1995 American Bible Society.

Scriptures quoted from the Good News Bible published by The Bible
Societies/HarperCollins Publishers Ltd, UK © American Bible Society 1966,
1971, 1976, 1992, used with permission.

A catalogue record for this book is available from the British Library

Printed in Singapore by Craft Print International Ltd

35 Stories
to make you
think

Heather Butler

Teaching values through RE

Dedicated to Derek.
Where would I be without you?

Contents

Life and death

Community life

Personal life

Foreword

Storytelling is such an important part of life as a teacher in primary school. Heather Butler is among the best. I remember very clearly sitting with the lead inspector during a school Ofsted inspection. He had observed Heather both teaching RE and leading an assembly and remarked, 'Heather has the art of getting right to the nub of the story.' He was, of course, absolutely right— I have seldom accepted a piece of inspection judgment so readily! Her art is no less evident in this collection of 35 wonderful stories.

Heather's stories remain a superb resource for PSHE, assemblies, circle times, small groups and work with individual children. To capture all 35 in a single edition makes this a teacher resource not to be missed. For me, though, the finest innovation in this particular volume is the addition of very clear links to RE teaching. The RE concepts picked up in each story alongside the Bible links and key verses ensure that these stories can be used very powerfully within the RE curriculum.

'The day the rain fell' struck a particular chord with me (it's incredible how many of the stories do just that). I recently experienced water cascading through the light fitting and on to the floor of my dining room—Heather has captured the ensuing chaos sublimely. The comparison with Carlos, a street child in Guatemala, really made me stop to think.

A word of warning: Heather's stories will have you thinking, laughing and crying in equal measure—they strike at the heart. Above all, they provide brilliant starting points for any RE teaching, as well as a host of other applications, and I would commend them to you.

Nick Waldron, Head Teacher, Hazlemere CE Combined School, Hazlemere, Bucks

Introduction

35 Stories to Make You Think is a compilation of the popular *Stories to Make You Think* series that addresses a range of topical and often sensitive issues relevant to the lives of children aged 6–10. It can be used on a one-to-one basis, in a group or with a whole class during Circle Time, PSHE, Citizenship, Religious Education or as part of an assembly.

Each chapter follows the same format and includes:

- A brief summary of the story.
- The RE concept that the story could be used to illustrate. The stories are suitable for helping children to apply what they have learnt about during an RE lesson and can be used as part of a plenary session. Each concept has suggested entry points to help explore children's understanding of the concept, a religious overview, a Christian viewpoint giving the Christian perspective, a key Bible verse and Bible story link.
- The story itself. Most of the stories are based on real life and all have been written in response to incidents that have occurred in the primary classroom. Each story takes between five and ten minutes to read.
- Comments that children have made after hearing or reading the story.
- Ideas to encourage children to think about the story.
- A thinking-time activity to follow up the ideas in the story.
- A prayer for use in a Christian context.

Family life

Families are special

Story summary

Jamie and Tom are twins. They live with their parents, younger sister Annie and Herbert the pet rabbit. The story follows a typical Saturday morning and explores how time is spent with family members. It raises issues about sibling rivalry, communication, the importance of doing things together and what can make family times special.

RE concept: Loyalty

 Exploring the concept

Children's understanding

- ❂ Explore what is the best thing about belonging to a family.
- ❂ Discuss what it means to be loyal.
- ❂ Talk about the identity that the family provides and how this relates to loyalty.

Religious overview

- ❂ Explore what it means to be part of a faith community and how members show loyalty to one another.
- ❂ In the Old Testament part of the Bible, Jewish law decreed that if a husband died, his brother should marry the widow. Discuss how this might have helped to maintain family groupings.

Christian viewpoint

Christians believe that God created human beings to live in community with him and each other. The Christian concept of the Trinity is based on 'family'—Father, Son and Holy Spirit—and the Church is seen as the worldwide family of God. In the Bible, the family is seen as the stronghold of the community and the best form of support for the individual.

Do children agree with this viewpoint?

 Key Bible verse

It is truly wonderful when relatives live together in peace.
PSALM 133:1

 Bible story link

In the Bible, there is the story of a young woman called Ruth who lived in the country of Moab. When her husband died, she lived with her mother-in-law, Naomi. Naomi's husband had also died. Eventually, Naomi decided to return to Bethlehem, the town where she had grown up, and suggested that Ruth stay behind in Moab. But Ruth showed her loyalty and how much she valued Naomi. 'I will go where you go, I will live where you live; your people will be my people, your God will be my God,' she said. They arrived in Bethlehem at harvest time. Ruth went to work in the fields, gathering corn. There she met Boaz, a relative of her first husband, who was the owner of the field. They fell in love and married and their child was an ancestor of Jesus' earthly father, Joseph. (Story synopsis based on Ruth 1:1—4:22.)

Saturday morning

Jamie and Tom are twins. They live in a house with their mum and dad, their pet rabbit Herbert and their little sister Annie.

Herbert officially lives in the garden, but comes into the house if the boys are with him. He likes the lounge carpet best. It tastes like cabbage. Annie is allowed in the house, too—and the garden, and her childminder's house. Dad lives at his office most of the time and comes home in the evening and at the weekends, when he sometimes visits the kitchen to put pizzas in the oven. Mum lives in the kitchen, but also hangs out at the school where she teaches, and the supermarket where she shops.

On the whole, life is not bad.

Jamie and Tom's favourite thing is football training on a Tuesday evening. Dad comes home early from work especially to take them. He takes them for a burger and chips afterwards. Their other favourite time is Saturday morning when Dad looks after Annie and Mum takes them swimming.

Today Annie and Dad are going to do some gardening together. Mum has said so. That means Dad will make himself a cup of coffee and read the paper while Annie pulls up some flowers and charges round the grass on her tricycle. Then Dad will get out the lawnmower and Annie will cry because she's scared of the noise it makes. So Dad will cheer and stop gardening.

Mum knows this will happen. Tom and Jamie know it will happen, too. They laugh about it in the car. Mum often has to work during the evenings, with marking and planning and things like that for school, so on Saturday mornings she is all ears to find out what the twins have been up to during the week. She wants to know what's happened at school, how their friends are, who they played football with, and anything else they want to tell her. Mum tells them about what she's been up to, too—how she dropped in to see Gran on Thursday and Gran wondered if they'd all like to go on holiday together this year.

'As long as we don't have to have Annie in our bedroom again,' Jamie says.

They are driving past the cinema. Tom fancies seeing one of the films advertised, but it's useless telling Mum because she doesn't like going to the cinema. He'll wait until they get home. Then he'll tell Dad.

Mum parks the car outside the swimming pool and fetches a ticket from the machine. 'There's just time to go to the shop,' she says, glancing at her watch. She buys herself a magazine and the boys choose a comic and a packet of sweets each. She always treats them exactly the same and makes a point of telling them so.

By ten o'clock, both boys are ready to start their swimming lesson. Mum is sitting on a bench watching them and reading her magazine at the same time. She knows she has half an hour to herself before she joins them in the water for a swim in the main pool. That is her exercise for the week.

Tom is really pleased today. Not only has he learned how to do a racing dive, but he also beats Mum in a race to swim twice up and down the pool.

'You're getting good,' she gasps as she tries to get her breath back.

Tom splashes her and swims off. He is extra pleased because he beat Jamie, too.

'Mum, have we got to go shopping?' Tom asks as they leave the pool three-quarters of an hour later. Sometimes they drop in to the supermarket on the way home. That is so boring. Today Mum shakes her head.

'I managed to get it all done last night,' she smiles.

'Yes!' Tom grins. He wants to read his comic and eat his sweets, not push a trolley and help decide which packets of cereal they will eat next week.

'Shall we go home, then?'

The boys nod. They like Saturdays.

Things children have said

'... mums get stressed before they even start taking the kids out and we have to put up with them getting cross with us when it's not our fault...'

'... you mustn't do something to embarrass your mum. That's terrible...'

'... I don't like my mum and dad watching me all the time. I like to be more grown-up and go places without them...'

'... the worst thing is when you have to behave yourself all the time if they take you some place you don't want to go to. That's dead boring...'

'... when our new baby came he had loads and she kept telling me to stop being jealous...'

'... if you're naughty then the others get a treat and you don't...'

'... I go fishing with the grey-haired guy who's my dad...'

Thinking time for children

Think about the people who are in your family. What do you like doing most with them? Do you ever spoil family times? Does anyone else in your family spoil them? Is there anything you can do to make family times better?

Thinking time activity

Draw your family on a piece of paper with you in the middle. Draw a line from you to each member of your family and on that line draw something you enjoy doing with them.

Prayer

Dear God, thank you for our families and the fun we have together. Thank you for the love we show each other. Help us to make family times really special. Amen

Moving to a new town

Story summary

Navdeep's father's new job means the family has to move—with the stress, loss and anxiety that that entails. The story confronts issues of moving, making new friends and looking after others in new surroundings.

RE concept: Finding security

 Exploring the concept

Children's understanding

○ Explore what moving to a new school would be like and share experiences of those who have actually done it.

○ Talk about what children would most miss if they had to move.

○ Talk about insecure feelings that children have. Order these feelings, with the most difficult to deal with at the top of the list.

Religious overview

○ Discuss how someone belonging to a faith community might be helped practically to find security in a new place—for example, with a ready network of friends and familiar symbols and rituals at their new place of worship.

Christian viewpoint

Christians believe that Jesus promised always to be with them and to give guidance and strength through the power of his Holy Spirit throughout their lives. In the Old Testament, before Jesus was born, the people of God believed that he guided and protected them in the same way.

Do children agree with this viewpoint?

 Key Bible verses

Jesus said, 'I will be with you always, even until the end of the world.'

MATTHEW 28:20

Your love is a treasure, and everyone finds shelter in the shadow of your wings.

PSALM 36:7

Bible story link

In the Bible there is a story about an Israelite girl who was captured by the Syrians and taken to be a slave in the house of Naaman, who was the commander of the Syrian army. Naaman had a dreadful skin disease, which is thought to have been leprosy. Far from home and in a foreign land, the Israelite slave girl had lost everything except her faith. However, she suggested to Naaman that he visit Elisha, the Israelite prophet, and ask to be healed. Eventually, Naaman went to see Elisha and was miraculously cured. (Story synopsis based on 2 Kings 5:1–14.)

Navdeep's nightmare

The idea of moving had all happened rather quickly. First of all, Dad had been offered a new job. Then he and Mum had gone away for a weekend while Navdeep stayed at Julie's. When they came back she was told that they had bought a new house where she would have a bigger bedroom to sleep in and a bigger garden to play in. They would be moving in three months' time.

Navdeep was supposed to be excited about it. Only she wasn't, and the nearer the time came to moving day, the less excited she felt. In fact, she was dreading it, and now there was only one day left. Tomorrow the removal firm would be arriving to load everything up into their great big van.

Navdeep slopped some milk on to the table. She had been aiming for her cereal bowl and missed. Mum told her to clean it up, in an irritated sort of way.

'I don't want to move,' Navdeep suddenly said as she wiped

the table. 'I want to stay here with my friends, but nobody ever asks me what I want to do.'

Mum sighed. 'Navdeep,' she said, 'we've been through this I don't know how many times already. Dad has to move with his job. If he doesn't work, we can't buy clothes or food or go on holiday or have a house or anything like that. So just accept it, will you? We are moving and that is that. You are getting a bigger bedroom and a bigger garden to play in—much bigger than I ever had when I was your age. And you'll soon make some new friends, you know that.'

Navdeep pulled a face. Not too much of a face in case Mum saw it and told her off again. Mum had told her off a lot lately. So she finished her breakfast and got ready for school. This year her teacher's name was Mrs Grasswell and she was really, really nice. Today, as Navdeep and Julie walked into the classroom, a girl they had never seen before was standing by the teacher's chair.

Mrs Grasswell looked up and smiled at them both. 'Hello, you two,' she said. 'I've got a special job for you. This is Amy who's come all the way from America and is joining our class. Could you look after her today and show her what to do?'

Navdeep looked at Amy. She did not look very happy, and now Mrs Grasswell was asking everyone to sit on the carpet while she took the register. Amy sat down between Julie and Navdeep. She went bright red and whispered in a strong American accent, 'Yes, Mrs Grasswell' when her name was called out.

'Can I go to the bathroom?' she then asked.

Mrs Grasswell said she could and asked Julie to go with her. As the door closed, someone started giggling.

'Is something funny?' Mrs Grasswell asked Nigel.

'That new girl talks funny.'

'And I expect,' Mrs Grasswell said, 'that to Amy, you talk funny, too. But Amy's not giggling at you, is she? She's got more sense. Now I'll have no more of it. We've all got to help Amy because it must seem very strange coming here.'

Navdeep suddenly wondered if she would sound different to everyone else when she moved. She had not thought of that before. If she did, she hoped no one would laugh at her.

The class lined up for assembly. Maths was straight after — fractions. Navdeep found those so hard.

She and Julie enjoyed showing Amy round the school, telling her what they were allowed to do at playtime and going through the names of all the teachers.

'We're allowed on the climbing frame on a Tuesday when it's Mrs Dawson's playground duty,' Julie said as they put their coats on.

Amy smiled. 'We didn't have a climbing frame like this at my last school,' she said, 'but we did have a swimming pool. We had one in our back garden as well.'

'If you get a sticker for doing good work,' Navdeep said, 'you have to go to Mrs Longford and she gives it to you.'

'Mrs Longford is the head teacher,' Julie added. 'She lives in the office with Mrs Jones the secretary. You have to take the register to her when it's your turn.'

'My old teacher used to give us a sticker if one of our teeth came out,' Amy said.

'You seem to be making new friends all right,' the dinner lady said to Amy as they filed into the dining hall at lunchtime. She went to fetch an extra chair so Amy could squeeze on to the same table as Julie and Navdeep. Then she turned to Navdeep.

'And you leave today, don't you? So Amy can have your seat tomorrow.'

The dinner lady had not meant to be unkind, but Navdeep suddenly felt sad because Julie would have Amy as a new friend instead of her. She did not like that thought and tried to put it out of her mind as they opened their lunch boxes.

'I'm going to email my best friend tonight,' Amy said as she took out an enormous sandwich. 'Her mum wants to know what this school is like.'

Navdeep looked at Julie. She would do the same—or phone, which would be even better. Mum had said she could if she wanted to.

At home time, Mrs Grasswell said 'goodbye' to Navdeep and gave her a present. It was a little book and everyone in the class had written their names on the front page. That was rather nice.

'Let's say a special prayer for Navdeep,' Mrs Grasswell said as she gave the little book to her. 'Dear God,' the teacher began, 'please be with Navdeep tomorrow as she moves. Keep her safe and help her make lots of friends in her new school. Amen.'

'Amen,' everyone repeated.

'We're going into town tonight,' Amy said as they lined up to leave the classroom. 'Mom said we'd get a pizza because she won't have unpacked all the cooking things yet.'

They collected their coats and bags from the cloakroom and walked out into the playground. A lady was standing just outside the door on her own. All the other mums were chatting by the school gate or milling round the playground.

'Hi, Mom, it was great,' Amy shouted out. 'That girl's called Julie and here's Navdeep and there's Janetta and Paula and my teacher's called Mrs Grasswell and there's the dinner lady who looked after us at lunchtime. She's Pete's mum, and Charlotte's having a party next week.' She paused for breath.

'OK, OK,' her mum said. 'And don't forget you've got to email Sonia tonight. You'll have a lot to tell her.'

Amy nodded and jumped up and down.

'Will I be like that?' Navdeep wondered as she stood in the

playground holding her PE bag and some books to take to the next school. She hoped so.

Mum was talking to Mrs Longford. 'I was just saying "goodbye" and "thank you",' Mum said.

'Well, Navdeep,' Mrs Longford smiled. 'The next few weeks will be full of new things, won't they? Remember, grown-ups are funny things. They don't always let children know what they're feeling inside. But that doesn't mean you don't have to tell them what *you're* feeling. If you're feeling sad, say something. Promise?'

Navdeep nodded.

'Mum,' Navdeep said as they walked home. 'Do you really want to move?'

Mum paused before she answered. Then she said, 'Put it like this. I'll be glad when the next few weeks are over. I don't want to leave all my friends and our house and the things we know here. It's hard work packing up and I'm very tired at the moment. But it's quite exciting to think about all the new friends we'll be making and all the new places there'll be to explore.'

'We had a new girl in our class today,' Navdeep said. 'She's going to have a pizza tonight. Can we?'

Mum looked at her daughter and smiled. 'Good idea,' she said. 'I can't face cooking and there's nothing much in the fridge anyway. We could even go to the Pasta House if you'd prefer.'

Navdeep thought about it for a moment. 'Can we get a pizza tonight and find a pasta place tomorrow?' she asked hopefully.

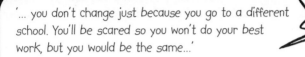

Things children have said

'... you don't change just because you go to a different school. You'll be scared so you won't do your best work, but you would be the same...'

'... she might think someone was going to steal her best friend from her as soon as she left...'

'... we moved and it was horrible. I cried all the way over here...'

'... we had to when Mum left Dad. I'm glad now because I've got lots of friends and I prefer living here than where we used to live...'

'... my mum was dead stressed and shouted at us. She shouted at Dad as well and he shouted back at her and I hid...'

'... the removal firm might leave her favourite toys behind...'

'... everything is safe where she is and it won't be safe at her new school...'

'... I'd show her what to do and let her come to my house...'

'... I'd tell her what the teacher and the dinner ladies are like. And everyone's names...'

'... the weather would be different if you moved to a different country...'

Thinking time for children

Think about a time when you had to go to a place you'd never been to before. Did you enjoy it? If so, why? If not, why not? Would everyone have felt the same as you did?

How can you help other people who have had to move to a place where you know everyone and where everything is?

Thinking time activity

Make a list of things you would do if a new person joined your class and you were asked to look after them. Then make a list of things you would want someone to do if you were the new person. Are they different or the same?

Prayer

Dear God, thank you that you are everywhere and that you are always with us wherever we go. Amen

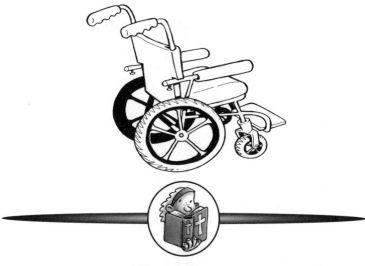

Disabled family member

Story summary

Following a car accident, Lee's brother Jason returns from hospital unable to walk. Life has changed for ever. When Lee goes on a school residential, he has time to reflect on the changes Jason's accident has brought. The story explores the impact a disabled family member can have on the lives of others and how all parties can be supported.

RE concept: Caring

 Exploring the concept

Children's understanding

- Discuss what we mean when we say someone has a disability and how a disability affects both the disabled person and those around them (not necessarily in a negative way).
- Explore how a caring community can offer support and care for those who need it.

Religious overview

- Explore how and why faith communities care for others.

Christian viewpoint

Christians believe that they are asked to care for others because this is the model Jesus has set by example in his life and teaching.

Do children agree with this viewpoint?

 Key Bible verses

'When I was hungry, you gave me something to eat, and when I was thirsty, you gave me something to drink. When I was a stranger, you welcomed me, and when I was naked, you gave me clothes to wear. When I was sick, you took care of me, and when I was in jail, you visited me... Whenever you did it for any of my people, no matter how unimportant they seemed, you did it for me.'

MATTHEW 25:35–36 and 40

 Bible story link

King Saul's grandson, Mephibosheth, was crippled in both feet. King David, who became king after Saul, asked, 'Are any of Saul's family still alive? If there are, I want to be kind to them.' King David's servants told him about Mephibosheth. From then on Mephibosheth ate at the king's table—a way of saying that David looked after him in every respect. (Story based on 2 Samuel 9:1–13.)

My brother is different now

Jason was in hospital for three months after the accident. Lee and Dad visited him most weeks. Mum stayed at the hospital. She had to give up her job to be with him.

'No holiday this year,' she said, 'but at least Jason's alive.'

Lee was angry. Why had that stupid woman got drunk and then driven into his brother as he cycled home from football training? Why hadn't she stayed at home? Why hadn't Jason stayed at home? Then none of this would have happened.

Once, when they went to the hospital, Dad had cried on the way home. Lee had cried, too. They had been told that Jason would never walk again. He would never ride his bike. He would never climb up on to the top bunk, or run, or play football. He was two years older than Lee and, at the age of twelve, he was confined to a wheelchair for the rest of his life.

'I want to write to Jason,' Lee said when they got home.

'That's a nice idea.'

'I don't know what to say.'

'He's still your brother. He can still think and talk and laugh like he used to. It's just that he can't walk. What would you write about if he wasn't in hospital?'

'I wouldn't, because he'd be here at home.'

Dad drew a deep, deep breath.

'Rotten, isn't it?' he whispered.

Lee nodded. He felt so helpless, so small.

'Why don't you tell him what you're doing next week and that you can't wait for him to come home again?' Dad suggested.

'OK,' Lee said. 'I'll also tell him how you burnt the fish fingers we had for tea last night.'

By the time Jason and Mum came home, the builders had been in and altered the house. The dining room was now Jason's room; the garage was a bathroom and storage area. Wheelchair ramps led up to the front and back doors, and Mum's brother, who earned lots of money, had paid for a brand new people-carrier.

Everything was done that could be done—for Jason. It was Jason this and Jason that. Lee did not mind at first. It was nice having Jason and Mum home again. After a while, though, it began to get on his nerves. Dad never came down to the park to kick a ball around with him. But he'd spend hours playing on the PlayStation with Jason.

❧

The weeks went by. Lee's class went on a school residential. Lee loved every minute of it. One morning his orienteering group had got completely lost and Mr Hickman had torn his Manchester United football shirt on a tree. Then they'd lit a fire and cooked sausages and marshmallows over the flames before going to the barn for their archery session.

Today it was raining. Most of his friends had decided to play cricket in the rain. Lee didn't fancy that, so instead he headed for the empty table next to the tuck shop. He had his notebook with him.

'Dear Mum, Dad and Jason,' he wrote, 'I'm having a brilliant time. Yesterday we went grass-sledging and were allowed to oil our own sledge wheels to make them go faster. Sledge number

5 was best. Then we went canoeing and one of the girls had a frog in her canoe and fell in the water. I fell in, too. One of the teachers hung our clothes up in the kitchen to dry.'

Someone was standing next to him.

'You OK over here on your own?' Miss Taylor asked.

Lee nodded. He liked Miss Taylor. She was more like a friend than a teacher.

'Who are you writing to?'

'My brother, and my mum and my dad.'

'How's your brother doing?'

'He's great.'

That was what Lee always said when people asked him how Jason was. Miss Taylor looked straight at him.

'And are you great?' she asked.

Lee said nothing. Dare he be totally honest? He had never told Mum or Dad how he really felt. They were too busy. He had never told them how tired he was of all the attention they gave Jason, or that sometimes he felt guilty because it was Jason and not himself who had been injured. He had never told anyone that.

'He's still Jason but he's different.'

There was a pause. Miss Taylor said nothing.

'Mum can't manage getting him in and out of the wheel-chair on her own, and she's done her back in, so I have to help move him around.'

'Do you mind that?'

Lee screwed up his face. He knew he ought to say he didn't. He ought to say he wanted to do everything he could to help his brother. But being away from home had made him realize just how different his life was now. Lee looked at the table.

'I taught a boy once,' Miss Taylor said, 'whose dad couldn't see properly. Phil had to do jobs round the house and help with the shopping and the cooking and the cleaning and loads of other things. He used to get really fed up about it.'

There was silence.

'Jason threw a cushion at Mum the other day. They both ended up screaming at each other. I phoned Dad at work and he came home early.'

'That was sensible,' Miss Taylor said. 'And do you get fed up and angry as well?'

Lee looked at the teacher.

'I don't hate him or anything,' he said. 'I just... well... I wish everything was like it used to be.'

'Everyone does, but that can never be.'

Lee didn't say anything. Someone had written 'I love Sparky' on the table in felt-tip pen. He studied the letters very closely and fought back the tears. 'I wish...' he began but got no further before he buried his head in his hands to hide his face.

'It's OK,' Miss Taylor said, putting her hand on his shoulder. 'You've been brilliant for so long. So brave. You looked after your dad when your mum was away and you've been fantastic with Jason since he's come home. Maybe it's time you looked after yourself.'

They stayed in the hall for quite a while. Children came in and out but no one bothered them.

'Are you going to buy a present for Jason when you go home?' Miss Taylor asked when Lee began to feel a bit better. He nodded.

'I've got Mum and Dad some of those chocolate fingers from the gift shop, but I don't know what to get Jason.'

'Get him something really wacky. Like...' She thought for a moment. 'A...'

Things children have said

'... disabled people are no different to anyone else, except they can't do everything...'

'... some disabled people can do loads more than people who have got everything...'

'... Lee's feeling disappointed, annoyed, wishing it had never happened, lonely because he used to play football with Jason, frightened in case he died...'

'... if you're in a wheelchair you can be yourself, go to the cinema, horse-riding and swimming, and there's a man on our estate who's got a special bicycle with an extra wheel so he can balance...'

'... disabled people win wheelchair races and compete in the para-Olympics or the London Marathon...'

'... there are lots of types of disabilities like spinal injuries, deafness, being slower at running than your friends, blindness, illnesses you get when you are born, when you hurt your arm and it goes in a sling, short arms...'

'... there's when you hurt yourself and can't use some part of your body for a while. Only you get better again so that's not a real disability...'

'... they can't get food out of the cupboard if the cupboard is high up...'

Thinking time for children

Do you know anyone who is disabled? What can they do? What can't they do? How can you help them? How can we as a community help them? Do we do enough? Should we call disabled people 'them' or are they 'us'? Can you think of anything you do that could make someone feel more disabled than they really are?

Thinking time activity

Make a list of as many 'disabling' things as you can think of, from being hard of hearing to breaking a finger. For each one, write down two things other people can do to help someone with that disability. What would be the worst thing someone could do?

Prayer

Dear God, thank you for our bodies and all the things they can do. Help us when we spend time with anyone whose body does not work as well as our own. Amen

Redundancy

Story summary

Helen returns from school to find her mum crying because she has been made redundant. The impact dawns over the next few months, not least because the promised skiing holiday is cancelled. The story explores how adults feel when they are made redundant and how children can help. It also raises issues about sacrificial giving.

RE concepts: Giving and self-worth

 Exploring the concept

Children's understanding

⚙ Discuss how children feel about themselves.

⚙ How do families and communities pull together and give to one another to get through difficult times?

⚙ Explore what giving means, especially when it results in denying yourself something you might want. This is known as sacrificial giving.

Religious overview

⚙ Discuss how a faith community could help restore a sense of feeling valued and loved.

Christian viewpoint

Christians believe that they should give one tenth of their earnings away to charities or others in their faith community who need it. This is seen as their gift back to God for all he has given them, even if it means they cannot have things they might want themselves.

Do children agree with this viewpoint?

 Key Bible verse

'People of Israel, every year you must set aside ten per cent of your grain harvest.'
DEUTERONOMY 14:22

 Bible story link

One day, Jesus was sitting in the temple near the offering box and watching people put in their gifts. People would give money to God by giving it to the temple. Rich people dropped in money—tiny amounts compared with what they owned—and made sure everyone could see how generous they were. Then a widow quietly dropped in two small copper coins. It was all she had and she had given it to God. This showed much about her commitment to God and that she was prepared to give sacrificially. (Story synopsis based on Mark 12:41–44.)

Winter break

Helen nearly choked on her mouthful of curry when Dad asked what she thought about going skiing next winter.

'Yeah!' she gasped. 'Holly goes every year and says it's brilliant.'

'Well, I went to the travel agent this morning,' Mum said with a huge grin on her face. She laid a brochure on the table. Snow, skis, snowboards, smiling faces, sun, hotels and huge plates of food looked up from glossy pages.

'Will it be cold?' James asked.

'Of course it will,' Helen said, without much kindness in her voice. James was so stupid sometimes.

'Helen!' Mum said. 'James is only five and just because you've been around four years longer than he has, you don't have to be rude to him.'

Helen stared at the tablecloth. She did not like being told off.

'We'll buy special ski-suits to keep ourselves warm,' Mum told James, 'so don't you go worrying about it.'

'It's a good thing Mum's working,' Dad laughed, 'with all the extra things we're going to have to buy.'

'It's going to be brill!' Helen whooped, the telling-off forgotten. 'When do we go?'

'It's May now and we'll go next February,' Mum said. She counted on her fingers. 'Nine months.'

'That's ages,' Helen sighed.

'It'll go fast enough,' Dad said. 'Now, I like the look of this hotel. Does anyone else?'

Helen looked at the photograph of The Charlotte Hotel in Austria. The symbols underneath showed that it had an indoor swimming pool, two restaurants, and ski lifts just a ten-minute bus ride away. 'Is that where we're going?' she asked.

'Maybe.'

❖

It was the beginning of October when Helen came home from school and found Mum and Dad in the kitchen. She knew something was wrong straight away. Dad should have been at work and then they stopped talking as she came through the back door. Mum had been crying.

'What's the matter?' Helen asked.

'Mum's been made redundant,' Dad whispered.

Helen frowned. She had heard that word before but was not quite sure what it meant.

'She's lost her job,' Dad added. 'She had to clear her desk and come straight home.'

'Sandra's been kept on,' Mum exploded, 'and I'm better than she is and she knows it. I didn't like the job anyway.'

Helen frowned again. Mum used to say how much she enjoyed it.

'You've got to see it as the job they've got rid of, not you as a person,' Dad sighed. 'And the people still working will have to do all you did as well as their own work, and I doubt if they'll get paid extra.'

'But at least they'll have a job and be earning some money,' Mum yelled. 'I won't. Those men in grey suits who get rid of

38

people like me, they're all right. They haven't gone home tonight without a job, have they?'

Dad looked at Helen.

'James is in the lounge,' he whispered. 'Can you keep him out of the way for a while?'

'OK,' Helen whispered back.

'Don't go in the kitchen,' she muttered to James.

'Why not?' he asked.

'Just don't. Mum and Dad don't want us in there.'

'But I want my tea.'

'Well, you can't have any yet, so you're staying here.'

After a while, James stood up.

'You are not going into the kitchen,' Helen said.

'I want Mummy and I want my tea.'

'Stick your thumb in your mouth and eat that instead.'

'I want Mummy,' James said, and looked as if he was going to cry.

At that moment they heard the shushing noise the freezer made when it was being shut.

'See, they're getting tea ready, so sit down.'

'I don't believe it,' Mum wailed from the kitchen twenty minutes later. 'I can't even cook a pie without burning it. I'm useless. That's why they got rid of me, because I'm useless.'

'No you're not,' Dad said. 'Calm down, will you?' He walked into the lounge.

'Do you two fancy fish and chips tonight? Because that's what we're having.'

❖

By the middle of December, Helen and James understood what Mum being redundant meant. It meant watching her fill in forms as she applied for jobs, and waiting for the postman each day in the hope that someone would write to her and offer her an interview. It also meant she got cross with Helen and James, sometimes for no reason at all. It meant renting a video instead of going to the cinema. It meant Mum losing weight and looking tired and—Helen kept noticing this—Mum did not smile as much as she used to.

On Christmas Day, there weren't as many presents as usual. Helen had asked for a ski-suit. She got a new jumper. It was a very nice jumper and she liked it, but it wasn't the pink and green ski-suit she had hoped for.

'What will I wear in February?' she asked.

Mum looked at Dad. Dad looked at the carpet.

'I'm sorry,' he said, 'we can't afford it any more.'

Helen bit her lip and tried to hide her disappointment.

'I'm sorry,' Mum added. 'It's my fault, but there's nothing I can do.' She had tears in her eyes as she said it.

'Holly's going,' Helen said. 'She's going to Switzerland.'

The first thing Mr Hopward told them about next term was a charity in Africa raising money to help farmers buy their own machinery.

'We're hoping to raise £500,' he told the school. 'We'll have cake stalls and a bring-and-buy sale in three weeks' time. And there'll be a sponsored skip. Your teachers will give you the forms tonight.'

Helen wasn't very happy taking her form home and giving it to Mum. Only that morning Dad had said he was going to think about cycling to work to save money. Mum read the information at the top of the form. Her face looked sad.

'You know what,' she said, 'we have so much.' Then she walked over to the drawer where she kept her purse. 'Here. I know you'll be able to skip for the full five minutes without stopping.' And she laid a £20 note on the table. 'I'd saved this and was going to treat myself to a new skirt. But I think you skipping and helping farmers grow food is more important.'

'But you haven't got a job,' Helen said.

'So? Neither have these farmers if they haven't got equipment. And anyway, I've applied for three jobs today and one of them pays more than I was getting before. If I get it we'll have cream cakes for tea. OK?'

Four weeks later, they ate cream cakes.

'There's a present for you on your bed,' Mum said as Helen licked her fingers.

Helen ran upstairs and opened the bright yellow carrier bag. Inside was something that was pink and green and...

'Mum, it's brilliant!' she shouted. 'But it's far too big for me.'

'You'll have grown a bit by February next year, won't you?' Mum laughed.

It was lovely to hear Mum laugh again.

Things children have said

'... mums and dads try to be brave in front of the children but they're not brave inside...'

'... Mum's money was so they could go on trips to theme parks and repair things in their house...'

'... adults don't always want you to know what they're talking about...'

'... they can help around the house, say nice things to Mum, be extra nice to each other, stay out of Mum's way, tell Mum they love her...'

'... I get scared in case it gets into an argument...'

'... Mum would be feeling depressed, annoyed, upset, angry that other people have still got their jobs and she hasn't, lonely and scared, wondering if she'll be able to find another job, useless...'

'... the best thing is for them to be themselves...'

Thinking time for children

If you had been working and then were told you wouldn't be needed any more, you might think you were useless and that no one valued you or wanted you. What would you do to remind yourself of how special you are and how other people do value you?

Thinking time activity

Divide a page into twelve sections and label one section for each of the coming twelve months. Draw the things you can look forward to each month that will not need any money spending on them. Who will be there with you in each of the pictures you have drawn? Will you being there mean that other people will also enjoy it more?

Prayer

Dear God, please help my mum/dad to find a job that they enjoy doing. Please help people who have to make important decisions to make good ones. Look after anyone who does not have a job at the moment. Amen

Having a
famous parent

Story summary

Ashley's father is a puppeteer and although Ashley is proud of him and sometimes helps with his puppet shows, it is very embarrassing when Dad comes to school during Book Week. The story tackles issues surrounding parents and the roles they play in the community.

RE concept: Belonging

 Exploring the concept

Children's understanding

- ✺ Talk about communities and organizations that children belong to.
- ✺ Discuss what belonging means for the children in terms of expectations and commitment.

Religious overview

- ✺ Discuss how belonging to a faith community gives members identity through shared beliefs and values.

Christian viewpoint

Christians believe that everyone has a part to play in the Christian community. The Bible uses the analogy of the human body to talk about the importance of belonging. It explains how everyone is important, whatever their role.

Do children agree with this viewpoint?

 Key Bible verses

Our bodies don't have just one part. They have many parts... If our bodies were only an eye, we couldn't hear a thing. And if they were only an ear, we couldn't smell a thing... He did this to make all parts of the body work together smoothly, with each part caring about the others. If one part of our body hurts, we hurt all over. If one part of our body is honoured, the whole body will be happy.

1 CORINTHIANS 12:14, 17 and 25–26

Bible story link

In the Bible there is a story about a famous father—King David—and his son, Solomon, who became king of Israel after David's death. During his lifetime, King David had prepared plans, finances and materials for Solomon to build a temple in the city of Jerusalem. Solomon's plans, however, far exceeded what David had imagined. The temple Solomon built was so lavish that it became a famous showpiece in the known world of his day. Solomon worshipped God as his father had done before him and God rewarded Solomon with the gift of wisdom. Solomon's wisdom made him a powerful, famous and well-respected king. (Story synopsis based on 1 Kings 1:1—8:66.)

Eek! It's my dad

Dad was making his lunch. A cheese and tomato roll, a packet of crisps, an apple, a yoghurt, a drink... and a nose.

'Is Estas having anything today?' Dad pondered.

Ashley laughed. 'Not today. He's not hungry.'

'Talking of Estas,' Dad said, 'can you help me load the van? I'm running a bit late.'

Dad unlocked the back door, crossed the patio and went into the den. Even though he was nine, Ashley still thought the den was the most magical place in the whole world, with all the old suitcases stacked against the far wall and the labelled plastic boxes piled up next to them.

On the left-hand side of the room was Dad's enormous workbench. This was where Dad created his puppets. There were moulded heads with flat noses lying on it today. Dad must be making friendly puppets. Pointed noses were for wicked trolls, like the one who lived in the brown suitcase with the green and purple skull painted on the outside. She ate children's eyes for breakfast. At least, that was what Dad told his audiences.

Today Dad was taking four puppets with him, including Estas. Ashley gently lowered the green suitcase to the floor.

'Have a nice day, Estas,' he whispered.

'Thank you, I will,' Estas whispered back.

'Ash,' said Dad in his own voice, 'I meant to ask you yesterday and forgot. I'm doing a show in half-term next week. Do you want to come and help me? It'll mean an early start.'

'With a long car ride?'

Dad nodded as he pulled his long hair back and tied it into a ponytail. Ashley wished he'd get it cut. No one else's father wore pink scrunchies in his hair.

On the following Tuesday, Ashley had to get up at half past six. Mum was in the kitchen looking half asleep. Nothing new in that. She gave him two packed lunches, one marked 'Ash' and one marked 'Dad'.

'You're in charge of those,' she grunted, 'and don't get them muddled up.'

'Have I got peanut butter?' Ashley asked.

'Yup, and I'm going back to bed for some more sleep,' she said. 'Have a good day.'

Dad was already outside, loading up the van. There were eight suitcases today, including the wicked troll and the beautiful princess who always spoke with a lisp. They had to fit the suitcases round props boxes, staging boards, lighting, sound cases and a hatstand. Last of all, Dad brought out a plastic box with little sticks, sponge balls, fabric and paints. They were for the workshop.

'Nasty puppets have dark colours, happy ones have bright colours and each has to be as light as possible so your arms don't get too tired. Even my arms with their tattoos and muscles get tired if the puppets are too heavy,' Dad said, mimicking himself as if he were up front introducing the workshop.

Ashley laughed. Today was going to be a good one.

They drove down the motorway and got lost when they came off the slip road, but eventually they found the hall where Dad was performing. A man with a worried look on his face greeted them.

'I thought you'd got lost,' he said.

'We did,' Dad said, 'but we're here now.'

Twenty minutes later, lots of children were sitting on the floor at Dad's feet, admiring his 'Peronski's Puppets' T-shirt. Ashley was behind the black screen, following Dad's script. For this part of the show he was in charge of the sound effects. The story was a Russian fairytale. An old soldier, who staggered under the weight of all the medals he had won in fierce battles, woke up one morning to find that his nose had fallen off. It made him different from everyone else, so he ran away.

Dad then pretended he was hungry and took out his lunch. He took a bite from the cheese and tomato roll and out popped... a nose.

'How did you get in there?' he asked the nose.

'I don't know,' the nose replied.

'I don't know who you belong to,' Dad said and tossed the nose high in the air so that it landed behind the black screen. Ashley caught it. Then he picked up a little nose puppet complete with hair growing out of its nostrils, and made it dance along the top of the screen while Dad put on a long skirt, old cardigan and grey wig. He was now the old lady who helped the soldier find his nose.

'So at last he is like everyone else and has his nose,' Dad

finished and everyone burst into applause.

'It's great having you to help me,' Dad said as they packed up at the end of the day. Ashley smiled. He thought his dad was brilliant, but he never told anyone at school exactly what his father did for a job in case they laughed at him.

No one else had a dad who was a puppeteer and ventriloquist. The letters 'b', 'm' and 'p' were the hardest sounds to make without moving your lips. Ashley knew that because his dad had told him, but he did not think anyone else would want to know. All the other dads seemed to work with computers or in offices, making lots of money. His dad did not. His dad was just different, not least because he had long hair tied back with pink scrunchies.

'My dad works in an office,' he would say, which was partly true because the den was a bit like an office.

❖

The following Thursday, at school, Ashley's teacher said they were going to have a treat. As part of Book Week, a Mr Peronski was waiting for them in the hall with some of his friends. Ashley was nearly sick. His dad, who dressed up as a woman and told stories in funny voices, was going to perform in his school! Everyone would laugh at him—that was for sure.

'Mr Peronski is a puppeteer,' said Mrs Jones, the head teacher, when everyone was sitting quietly, 'and I'm sure we're all going to enjoy watching him.'

'And I am Mr Peronski,' Dad said, emerging from behind the black screen. He spoke in a Russian accent and wore an old hat and a thick coat with a huge collar. Ashley closed his eyes and wished he were anywhere but here. Even going to the supermarket with Mum would be better than this.

Suddenly Laura whispered from behind him, 'That's your dad, isn't it?' Ashley decided to ignore her and pretend the waistcoat and long hair, the fancy earrings and funny voices weren't happening. And Dad's mouth did move a little bit when the puppets were talking. What were they all thinking?

Laura shuffled her feet and undid the Velcro fastening on her shoes. Ashley wanted to turn round and tell her to sit still. He wanted her to think his dad was brilliant.

Everyone was laughing and giggling. 'They're laughing and giggling at him,' Ashley thought. 'They think he's useless.' But they were laughing *with* him, and that was different. That was all right. They laughed with him because they thought he was good.

'I need someone to help me,' Dad said. Lots of people put their hands up. 'You, there,' he said, pointing at Ashley, 'would you come and help me?'

There was a sigh of disappointment from those who had wanted to be chosen. Ashley stood up and went to the front. Dad grinned at him. 'Can you do the nose job for me?' he whispered as they went behind the screen together. Of course he could.

At the end, everyone clapped so loudly and for so long, Ashley thought he was going to burst with pride. He stood next to his dad and looked up at him. His dad was the best dad in the world, even with his pink scrunchies.

'There's someone here,' Mrs Jones began as the applause died down, 'who had a big shock this morning. For those of you who don't know, Mr Peronski is Ashley's dad.'

Ashley blushed.

'Do you like having a famous dad?' Mrs Jones asked him.

'Sort of,' Ashley called back.

Mrs Jones spoke to the whole school.

'I expect lots of you have got puppets lurking in cupboards that you'll get out tonight,' she said. 'Well, Ashley's got... how many?'

'Seventy-two.'

'And which is your favourite one?'

'Estas,' Ashley said, without hesitation.

'Why do you like that one?'

'Because that's the one I helped Dad to make when I was little,' Ashley said, and blushed again.

'You're a very lucky boy,' Mrs Jones said, and suddenly Ashley knew he was.

At lunchtime, Ashley opened his lunch box. Inside was a peanut butter sandwich, an apple, a yoghurt and... the spare nose puppet with hair sticking out of its nostrils. He picked it up.

'I would like you to meet,' he said in a Russian accent, 'I would like you to meet the running nose. And how, my friends, does a monkey smell if it loses its nose? Yes, it smells terrible.'

Everyone laughed out loud and the dinner lady came over to see what was going on.

'D'you want to be like your dad?' she asked.

'Maybe,' Ashley said, 'but I'm not absolutely sure.'

'You want to be yourself, don't you?' she said.

'Yes,' Ashley agreed. 'I do.'

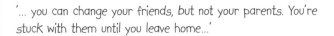

Things children have said

'... when you are bullied you feel different. It makes you feel left out. You need your family then. Bullying stops you belonging to other people because you feel so bad. It's horrible...'

'... you can change your friends, but not your parents. You're stuck with them until you leave home...'

'... my mum embarrasses me when she tells me to have a bath in front of my friends and makes me kiss someone...'

'... sometimes she's silly in front of my friends and the clothes she wears do my head in. I have to walk in front of her and hope we don't meet anyone I know...'

'... I was at a presentation for footy and I was the only one in smart clothes that my mum had made me wear...'

'... my mum is the lollipop lady outside our school. That's different, but I don't mind because she's like that anyway and everyone likes her...'

'... my dad sings in the shower. No one else's dad does that as far as I know and it's awful when my friends come round...'

'... my mum does people's nails at a health centre and calls herself a nail technician. I never tell anyone. I say she's a fitness instructor...'

Thinking time for children

What is the best thing about belonging to your family? Does being with your family ever make you feel awkward? What are the good things you do together? Which other groups do you belong to and why?

Thinking time activity

Write down four embarrassing things your parents and family have done and share them with a friend. Now put them in order, with the most embarrassing one at the top. You are part of and belong to that family, and that family belongs to you.

For everything you've written down, say what the result of each has been. Did it bring your family closer together? Did it make you secretly proud of belonging to your family? Is it still an embarrassment? If the latter, will it always be embarrassing?

Prayer

Dear God, thank you for my parents, even though they sometimes do some strange things I wish they didn't. These are the things I don't like them doing ....
Help me to cope with them. Amen

A parent remarries

Story summary

Joey dislikes Adam and Selina, who are his mum's boyfriend's children. He's not too keen on Uncle Dave, either, but Mum wants them all to be one big happy family. The story raises issues about what happens when parents separate and then find new partners with resulting new relationships, as well as the possibility of moving house and the ensuing jealousy as parents welcome other children into the new family unit.

RE concept: Forgiveness

 Exploring the concept

Children's understanding

✪ Discuss with the children how broken relationships affect other people and how, with care, time and forgiveness, new and stronger relationships can be made.

Religious overview

✪ Explore how forgiving people can be very difficult, but is central to mending broken relationships.

Christian viewpoint

Christians believe that they should not judge other people and should be prepared to forgive things done or said against them. In this way, Christians reflect the grace God shows when he forgives them.

Do children agree with this viewpoint?

 Key Bible verse

Put up with each other, and forgive anyone who does you wrong, just as Christ has forgiven you.
COLOSSIANS 3:13

 Bible story link

In the Bible, Jesus uses a story picture of birds and flowers to teach us not to worry about everyday things in life. He says that God our heavenly Father knows what we need even before we ask and that if we do as God wants, then everything else will follow. This story is a helpful illustration of how we should be accepting of life and of others, confident in the knowledge that those who love us will know how to look after us. (Story synopsis based on Matthew 6:25–34.)

I don't want to go to the cinema

Joey's dad left him and his mum when Joey was seven. A few years later, Joey's mum wanted to marry someone else. Joey found that very hard. He had got used to having his mum all to himself and he couldn't stand Uncle Dave's two children.

Joey sat very still and looked at the posters on his bedroom wall. He was trying to take in what Mum had just told him… that she and Uncle Dave were going to get married and, when they did, he and she would go and live in Uncle Dave's house with Uncle Dave's horrible children. Mind you, Mum had not called them horrible—she had said they were lovely and just needed a mum and a big brother like Joey.

A lot had happened over the last few years. First of all, there had been Dad walking out after he and Mum had had the most enormous row. When that happened, Joey had run up to his bedroom and buried his head under his quilt cover. He could still remember it.

Joey had hardly seen his dad since then. They had been to the park and the burger bar and the cinema several times. Joey had enjoyed that. He had asked Dad once if he was ever coming back home. His dad had said no way, if his mum was still there, and that he hated her.

Then Joey's dad stopped coming to see him. Mum said he had gone to live a long way away. Joey had never stayed at Dad's new flat, or gone on holiday with him, or been go-karting, or done any of the other things he had been promised they would do together.

At first Joey really missed his dad, but gradually he and Mum learned to live on their own. Mum got a job at the supermarket and said she could manage quite well by herself, thank you very much. She no longer needed his dad.

And then Uncle Dave turned up. Mum met him at work. Joey liked him all right and it was nice to have someone to kick a football around with in the garden. They would go to the video shop together and have a laugh, and Uncle Dave always bought him a huge packet of sweets. He was doing his best to make Joey like him. The bike at Christmas had been all right, too.

And then today had happened and he and Mum would soon be living with Uncle Dave and those two horrible children.

'I don't want to live with them,' was the first thing Joey said.

'Why not?' Mum asked.

'Because they play with my toys and break them,' he said.

'Not all the time, surely,' Mum sighed.

'They do,' Joey thought, remembering his Lego castle that little Adam had pulled apart last time he had been there.

'But Uncle Dave loves me,' Mum said. 'And you,' she added. 'He thinks the world of you. And you can call him Dad if you want.'

'I don't want to and I don't want *them* anywhere near me,' Joey blurted out. 'Why do *they* have to come?'

Mum sighed and kissed the top of his head. 'They're all right, you know. I spent yesterday evening with them,' she said, 'when you were round at Chris's.'

Joey pulled away from her. He had been hurting before, but suddenly he hurt even more.

'Did you tell them before me?' he shouted.

Mum glanced at her watch. 'We told them last night,' she said. 'They were really excited about it—and so will you be when you've had time to get used to the idea. It's going to be lovely for all of us. Now, we're off to the cinema in five minutes, so we'd better get ready.'

Mum had let him down like never before. She had told Selina and Adam about her and Uncle Dave before she had told him! Did she already love them more than him? He suddenly hated her and his real dad—and Uncle Dave.

Uncle Dave's house had three bedrooms. Which one would he have? Would he be allowed to put his football posters up? What would happen if Adam or Selina broke any of his toys? Would he tell Mum or would he tell Uncle Dave? Would Uncle Dave be nicer to them than he would be to him? Would Mum be nicer to them? What would happen if he wanted to watch one television programme and they wanted to watch a different one?

There were two of them and only one of him—only one. He was going to be all on his own. And they'd expect him to be good and play with the little ones while Mum looked after everyone—except him.

Then a thought came to him. Maybe if he tried extra hard to be good, Mum would love him more than the others. At least he had her to himself this afternoon. Right, he was ready. He had just reached the top of the stairs when the front door bell rang. Mum went to open the door.

'Dad says we're to start calling you Mum,' a little voice called out.

'Hello, Adam,' Mum said and bent down to kiss him. Then she leaned over and kissed Selina, who was in Uncle Dave's arms. 'Why are they here?' Joey thought.

'Hi there,' Uncle Dave called out. 'Are you ready? We must get a move on, or we'll be late. Selina and Adam have wanted to see the new cartoon film for ages.'

'I thought it was just me and Mum going to the cinema,' Joey stammered. 'I wanted to see the dinosaur film.'

'I know, darling,' Mum said, 'but that wouldn't be suitable for Selina and Adam, and we're going to the cinema this afternoon to be one big happy family and sit together.'

'But...' Joey began to say. 'What about me? Don't I count any more?'

'Joey,' Uncle Dave called out, 'I'd like to see the dinosaur film, too. Perhaps I could take you and some of your friends to see that later on?'

Things children have said

'... children should be told what their mums and dads are doing. Moving in with other children is horrible. I like them now, though...'

'... when they shouted at each other I used to run out of the door and go and play outside...'

'... I wish I was brave enough to shout "Stop it" at them but I'm not. My big sister wouldn't do it either...'

'... they don't shout at each other when we're around but sometimes they don't speak to each other and you know they've had a row and they think we don't know but we do because you can tell from the way they look at each other...'

'... Joey should have been asked if he wanted to live with them...'

'... he wouldn't like it. He'd cry and be lonely and his mum would have to come upstairs and look after him...'

'... I'd have legged it back upstairs as fast as I could and shut the door...'

'... I'd have gone, and done everything Mum wanted...'

'... it'll take ages but they might be happy together if everyone tries hard...'

'... I always hide underneath my quilt and hold my teddy bear very tight. I hate it when they shout. Sometimes he throws something at her and she screams at him...'

Thinking time for children

Think about one person in your family and a time when you fell out with each other. How did you become friends again and what did it feel like? What was the most important thing you had to do to make up?

Thinking time activity

Think of one good thing that everyone you live with does—like taking you swimming, or playing football with you, or smiling at you. Tell a partner the names of everyone you live with. Act out a time when you've been forgiven and a time when you have done the forgiving. Your partner has to guess what had happened.

Prayer

Dear God, sometimes things happen that we don't like and cannot change. Thank you that you have promised always to be with us and love us whatever happens. Amen

Living with separated parents

Story summary

Hayley's mum and dad have split up. She sees her dad at weekends. Just before Christmas he takes her on a real treat—a ride in a small aeroplane. Near where they land is a garden centre where he buys Christmas tree lights and an angel for the top of the tree. The garden centre gives them an Advent candle, which Hayley renames an *advert* candle. This story is an entry point to talk about coping with Christmas and other special occasions when families are split, and also about accepting difficult things that once hurt.

RE concept: Acceptance

 ## Exploring the concept

Children's understanding

⚙ Talk about circumstances that children have faced when they have had to accept something difficult—for example, a pet dying, or losing something precious.

⚙ Talk about how they came to terms with what had happened.

⚙ Talk about who helped them through this experience.

⚙ Explore whether the feelings of hurt and pain reduced as time passed and whether sometimes they still come back.

Religious overview

⚙ Explore how faith communities help people who are facing difficulties.

Christian viewpoint

Christians believe that God holds everything in his hands and has plans for their lives. Christians believe that people can never fully understand the mind of God, or why bad things happen to them, but they can be safe in the knowledge that God is with them in difficult times, even if *they* feel far away from him.

Do children agree with this viewpoint?

 ## Key Bible verses

God makes everything happen at the right time. Yet none of us can ever fully understand all he has done, and he puts questions in our minds about the past and the future. I know the best thing we can do is always to enjoy life.

ECCLESIASTES 3:11–12

Bible story link

In the Bible, there is a story about a young wife called Hannah. Hannah longed for a baby, but for many years she remained childless. In her day, this was seen as a disgrace and caused her great pain. In her distress, she asked God to give her a child and promised that if God answered her prayer, she would dedicate the child to him. Shortly afterwards, she conceived and gave birth to a baby boy, whom she named Samuel.

When Samuel was about three years old, Hannah took her son to the temple and dedicated him to God, just as she had promised. Samuel grew up in the temple under the care of Eli the priest and, later, became a great and much-respected prophet of God. Although Hannah visited her son each year, Samuel never again lived at the family home in nearby Ramah. (Story synopsis based on 1 Samuel 1:1—2:21.)

Aeroplane angel and the advert candle

Hayley's dad works at the hospital and lives in a house near the football ground. Hayley's mum works in a school and lives in a flat near the petrol station. And Hayley? She sees her dad every other weekend.

'I'll pick her up at eight o'clock tomorrow night,' Mum says. Dad smiles and nods his head. At least they don't argue like they used to.

'We're going to buy a Christmas tree,' Dad says. There is a twinkle in his eye. That means they will be doing something else as well.

'Where are we going, then?'

'I've told you. We're buying a Christmas tree.' Dad winks. There's more to this than meets the eye.

They drive for half an hour, chatting all the time. The engine of a small aeroplane buzzes overhead.

'See that plane?' Dad says, leaning forward to get a better view. 'That'll be us in a few minutes.' His grin is so big, his gums are showing. Hayley's stomach tries to tie itself into a knot.

'W… w… we're going up in one of those tiny little planes to buy a Christmas tree?' she stammers.

'Yup!' Her stomach pulls the knot tight as Dad turns into a little road leading to a flying club. A short man with a slight limp walks towards them as Dad parks the car.

'There's John,' Dad says, and waves. 'He's a friend of mine and flies planes for a hobby.' Hayley has never heard Dad talk about John before, but he is grinning at her.

'You must be Hayley,' he says. 'Ready for a spin? I've done all the checks and we're ready to go.'

A spin? Hayley is nearly sick. She's not sure if it's with excitement or fear.

'Here's where the Piper Warriors are all parked,' John tells them as they walk behind a row of five planes. 'You can fit two adults in the front, one child and one Christmas tree in the back.'

He helps Hayley climb on to the wing, slide into the back, fasten the seat belt and plug in her headphones. Dad and John strap themselves in the front.

'Clear prop!' John shouts, and the plane shudders as the engine surges into life. The control tower clears them and they taxi on to the runway—faster, faster, up, up, lurching and bumping. The roar of the engine fills her ears, but they're up, off the ground, and she can see someone walking across a field and a dog racing ahead, and there's a house with a blue cover over its swimming pool, and cars travelling slowly along a main road.

She is so small in this enormous clear blue sky with only one small cloud miles away. Is this what a bird feels like? The plane is levelling off and it's steadier now, not so bumpy. Her heart, too, is not racing so fast.

They land 25 minutes later.

'Did you enjoy that?' John asks.

'It was brilliant!' is all she can say.

'And the Christmas trees,' John laughs, 'are in the garden centre across the road from the airfield. I came here last year for mine.'

They choose a small tree—it has to be small to fit in the plane—some decorations and a new set of fairy lights. Hayley spots an angel with shining gold and silver wings. It is half-price because the left wing is damaged.

'Can we get this for the top of the tree?' she begs. 'We can mend the wing with glue and she'll be all right in the plane because she's used to flying.'

'She'll be an aeroplane angel, then,' Dad says, 'who eats African apples and… amazing artichokes at… afternoon tea.'

Hayley laughs. Her dad is funny sometimes.

'You've spent 40 pounds and 55 pence,' the lady at the counter tells them, 'so you get a free Advent candle. I'll slip it in the bag for you.'

It is a squash in the back of the plane. The tree branches wave and bounce as the plane cuts through the air. Aeroplane angel is perched on Hayley's arm, watching the shadows that the fences and trees make as the plane rises high into the sky.

Hayley suddenly wonders if real angels have flying lessons. Do they get hungry? Do they enjoy telling people amazing news, as they did when baby Jesus was born? Do they get injured if they have a crash landing? She looks at aeroplane angel. Aeroplane angel looks back at her, but says nothing.

It only seems like a few minutes before they are back at the flying club's airfield.

'We'll decorate the tree when we get home,' Dad says as they load it into the boot of the car. Hayley and Mum decorated their tree last week. Dad's will be different, though, because aeroplane angel will be at the top.

'I'll see you on Monday, then, Carl—and nice to meet you, Hayley.' John smiles. Hayley nods. 'Thank you,' is all she can say. She always runs out of things to say when an adult she doesn't know speaks to her.

They stop off for burgers and chips and then the super-market to buy Dad some food for next week. It is five o'clock by the time they get home. An hour later, aeroplane angel's wing is mended and she is perched on top of the Christmas tree.

'Can we open our presents?' Hayley asks. 'I've got yours in my bag. I brought them with me just in case.' She wants to add that she wished he and Mum would get together again, even if it was just for Christmas Day. But she doesn't. Mum told her she and Dad will never do that and she must not talk about it again. She must accept it. They both love her, but not each other.

'It's not Christmas Day yet!' Dad says.

'I know, but you're working at your smelly old hospital on Christmas Day, so I won't see you. Please!'

She makes him open the presents she has brought for him first—the calendar she made at school and a new tie she saved up for. He is admiring the tie when they are plunged into total darkness. The Christmas tree lights, the hall light, the main lights and the street lights all go out and the fridge-freezer in the kitchen stops whirring.

'Whoooah!' Dad says. 'That's a power cut. Where's that Advent candle? Good thing we spent so much money this morning.'

'It's by the glue on the table, I think.'

Dad feels his way into the kitchen and searches for some matches. Gentle light flickers on the walls as he returns. Carefully, he melts the bottom of the candle, sets it on a saucer and lights the wick at the top, making shadows dance on his face.

'We had an Advent candle at school when I was in Year 3,' Hayley giggles. 'I thought it was an advert candle.'

'Advert?'

'Like they have on the telly.'

'You are funny!' Dad says.

'Well, they didn't have tellies when Jesus was born, but they did have things like candles, so I thought that was what it was for. Someone lit a candle in the darkness and did an advert for something while everyone watched. Dad, do angels have flying lessons before they're sent to go and tell people things?'

'Hayley, I can't keep up with you! I've no idea, but I'll tell you something they didn't have when Jesus was born.'

'What?'

'They didn't have decorations, or cards, or Christmas trees, or presents.'

'Or adverts.'

'Or Advent.'

'Not Advent?'

'Well, Mary and Joseph had Advent, because Advent is about getting ready for Christmas and they got ready for their baby to be born.'

Hayley's present is in her dad's wardrobe. He takes the candle and fetches it. She rips off the sticky tape and paper to reveal a small leather box. Carefully, she opens it. Inside is a silver necklace with a single pearl.

'I wanted to give you something special,' Dad says. 'Something that will last.'

Hayley undoes the clasp and lays the necklace round her neck. She does not need a mirror to know how beautiful it looks. Dad's jumper is soft against her cheek as she gives him a hug.

'Thank you,' she says. 'It's lovely.' At that moment the lights come back on, the fridge-freezer starts whirring and the Christmas tree lights twinkle once more.

'Shall I blow the advert candle out, now?' Hayley asks. Dad smiles.

'Leave it burning,' he says. 'It will remind us that Christmas is nearly here.'

'Aeroplane angel could fly round the world now her wing's mended, and do an advert telling everyone to get ready for Christmas,' Hayley says.

'And would you like to fly with her?'

'Of course!'

'And what would you tell everyone?'

Hayley whispers something in his ear.

'I like that,' he whispers back.

Things children have said

'... my dad and my mum fight, but they don't split up...'

'... you don't really know what they're arguing about and they go on and on and on...'

'... you get scared, especially when they start screaming and swearing...'

'... all sorts of worries go through your head. My aunt and uncle argued and we didn't see them for years...'

'... if you have two houses to live in, you have more space and two lifestyles and each parent spoils you and it can be OK after a while...'

'... you'd have to keep moving and you wouldn't know where you were. It'd be very confusing...'

'... you need to see your parents together...'

'... I lost things and forgot things, then I got told off even more...'

'... if I was telling the world about Christmas, I would tell everyone to look after people you love...'

'... families need looking after...'

Thinking time for children

What is the best thing about the family unit(s) you belong to?

Thinking time activity

Make a list of things you like doing with your family and then with your friends. Are there things that are in both lists? Would you like to add something that isn't there at the moment? If you were going to get married tomorrow, what would you want your partner to be like?

Prayer

Dear God, mums and dads sometimes argue. Help me to be really strong if I hear them, and help them calm down and sort out what they're arguing about. Amen

Life and death

The death
of a pet

Story summary

When Fidget the hamster dies, Toby asks questions about death. His family share his loss and help each other to come to terms with what has happened. The story covers the stages of initial grieving and suggests ways to support and help someone facing bereavement.

RE concept: Feelings

 Exploring the concept

Children's understanding

⚬ Talk about children's experiences of losing pets and how it made them feel.

⚬ Talk about things people said and did that were helpful or unhelpful.

⚬ Explore how children feel about their loss now, and how their feelings have changed since the loss occurred.

⚬ Discuss whether it is right to show other people you are upset and talk about your feelings.

Religious overview

⚬ Explore how different religions set times for grieving and mourning.

Christian viewpoint

Christians believe that, through his life, death and resurrection, Jesus has opened the way for people to have eternal life after their physical death. Through the birth of his Son (the incarnation), God became fully human and yet was also fully divine. Because of Jesus, God understands people's pain in times of loss and sadness.

Do children agree with this viewpoint?

 Key Bible verses

God loved the people of this world so much that he gave his only Son, so that everyone who has faith in him will have eternal life and never really die.

JOHN 3:16

'God set [Jesus] free from death and raised him to life. Death could not hold him in its power.'

ACTS 2:24

Everything on earth has its own time and its own season. There is a time for birth and death… for crying and laughing, weeping and dancing.

ECCLESIASTES 3:1–2 and 4

 Bible story link

One of Jesus' close friends, Lazarus, was very ill. When he died, Jesus went to visit the family. Lazarus' sister ran to meet Jesus as he approached the house. 'Lord,' she said, 'if you had been here, my brother would not have died!' The Bible records that when Jesus saw her weeping, his heart was touched and he was deeply moved. He, too, wept openly. Then Jesus brought Lazarus back to life. (Story synopsis based on John 11:1–44.)

I'm going to miss you, little friend

Fidget was Toby's hamster. He was very sweet, very loved and always listened to everything that was whispered in his ear.

Every Saturday—well, nearly every Saturday (somebody else had to do it if he was too busy)—Toby changed the sawdust in Fidget's cage and cleaned out his little plastic house.

Each night—well, most nights (somebody else had to do it when he forgot, which was quite often)—Toby would make sure Fidget had enough food and water for the next day. He would open the cage door and hold out his hand. Fidget would run on to his hand to be taken downstairs to run around and be fed seedless green grapes that Mum had bought especially for him.

Fidget was part of the family.

One day, Toby bought Fidget a little wooden tube to climb in and out of, but Fidget never really used it. In fact, as Toby said to Mum a few days later, he hardly ever came out of his house these days.

'How long do hamsters live for?' Toby asked.

'About two years,' Mum answered.

'How long have I had Fidget?' he whispered, though he knew the answer already.

'About two years,' Mum said.

She did not say anything else. Neither did Toby.

It was a Sunday when Dad suggested checking Fidget's cage. There had been no sound at all from him since Friday night and Dad was a bit worried. Dad lifted the cage on to the floor, but no little whiskers twitched or wet nose poked out between the bars.

'He can't be dead,' Toby said in a brave sort of voice. 'I changed his water last night.'

'He hasn't touched it, though, has he?' Dad said as he gently lifted up the cottonwool bedding in the little plastic house.

Toby was glad Dad was there when he saw the still ball of fur lying inside it. He put his head on Dad's lap.

'Why did Fidget have to die?' he sobbed.

Dad did not answer because there was nothing to be said. All living things have to die, but telling that to Toby at the moment would not help at all. Instead, Dad whispered, 'It's all right to cry.'

He brushed away his own tears and stared at Fidget's little brown body, longing for it to move. But it did not. Fidget was gone—for ever.

Dad stayed with Toby until he stopped crying.

'There are few animals that were so loved,' Dad whispered.

'He was a very lucky hamster to have you to look after him.'

Eventually they put the cage, with Fidget still in it, back on the shelf where he had lived for the past two years.

'When you're ready,' Dad said, 'we'll bury him. But he can stay here for now.'

Several times during that day, Toby checked Fidget's cage. He wanted to make sure he was still there. He asked Dad if it was all right to pick him up, even though he was dead. Dad said he could as long as he washed his hands afterwards.

Somehow the rest of the day passed. Whenever Toby tried to think of something else, he couldn't. His chest felt tight as well and his tummy had a funny sort of ache inside it.

He did not sleep very well that night. He even got out of bed once and shone his torch into the cage. But Fidget did not come out and say 'hello' in the way he used to before. When he woke up, the first thing he did was to think of Fidget.

Toby was not looking forward to going to school, even though Mum had written a note telling his teacher about what had happened.

'Lots of your friends have had hamsters and other pets that have died,' she said, 'so they'll know how you're feeling.'

'I'm not going to cry, though,' Toby said. 'It's not cool to cry.'

'It might not be cool,' Mum commented, 'but it's sensible.' Then she added, 'If you need me, ask your teacher to phone and I'll come and get you, OK?'

Toby nodded and ran his hand over the photograph of Fidget he had put in his pocket. He wanted to have it with him to remind himself of what Fidget had looked like.

Mum smiled at him. It was a sad sort of smile. She hadn't slept very well, either. She had woken several times in the night, waiting to hear the noise Fidget used to make when he was snuffling round his cage. But all she had heard was silence.

'Right,' she thought. 'We'll have Toby's favourite pizza for tea to try to cheer him up.' So during her lunch break she went to the supermarket, fighting back the tears when she passed the seedless green grapes. 'This is stupid,' she tried to tell herself. 'He was only a hamster.' But he was Fidget the hamster, and that made him special and part of the family, and a great wave of sadness swamped her.

She told Toby about it when he got home from school. It helped him to know that someone else was finding it hard as well. Then he told her how his friends had looked after him at school and told him all about when their pets had died and what they had done and how they had felt. Mum was pleased that they had looked after him.

Life did not stop just because a hamster had died and, although Toby was still upset, the pain did begin to get less as the days went by. On Wednesday night, as he got ready for bed, he looked at Fidget for the last time. The following morning he asked Dad to take the cage downstairs.

'Do you want to bury him in the garden?' Dad asked.

'Not yet,' Toby whispered.

'That's fine,' Dad said. 'We'll leave him in the shed until you're ready.'

'OK,' he whispered.

It would not be long now before he was ready to say his final 'goodbye'. Toby knew that and so did Dad.

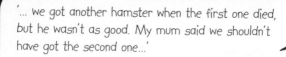
Things children have said

'... we got another hamster when the first one died, but he wasn't as good. My mum said we shouldn't have got the second one...'

'... we stuck the goldfish down the loo. I wouldn't go for ages in case it came back up and bit my bottom...'

'... we dressed up and did a proper service for my cat. She was called Snowy. My dad made a cross and we stuck it on top of her in the ground...'

'... I had a hamster, but the next day she was dead. I cried...'

'... I got cross and all upset and my little brother came and I shouted at him to go away...'

'... some people try to be brave, but they cry when they get home...'

'... we made a grave when our rabbit died. I cried all the time for ages...'

Thinking time for children

Think about your pets and what they mean to you. What feelings do you have when you think about them?

Thinking time activity

Draw a picture of your pet and write feelings associated with him or her round it. Now draw some pictures of memories

76

of things you have done with your pet. Maybe you have a photograph as well. Slip the paper in an envelope and put it somewhere safe. You might think of more memories that you can add later on.

Prayer

Dear God, thank you for all our pets and the love they give us. Help us always to look after them properly. Amen

Going to a funeral

Story summary

Sam doesn't want to go to his grandfather's funeral. However, he does go, and on the way he reflects on the events of the past few days as his parents explain what will happen at a Christian funeral service. The service and wake are then seen through Sam's eyes. The story raises questions and seeks to allay fears about death and the immediate feelings after someone has died.

RE concepts: Loss and afterlife

 Exploring the concept

Children's understanding

- Talk about experiences that children have had of people dying.
- Discuss how someone could be helped through this difficult time.

Religious overview

- Explore the beliefs that different religions have about the afterlife.

Christian viewpoint

Christians believe that life after death has been achieved through the life, death and resurrection of Jesus Christ, whom they believe to be the Son of God. By coming back to life, Jesus defeated death and opened the way for people to be able to have eternal life with God for ever.

Do children agree with this viewpoint?

 Key Bible verse

Jesus said to his disciples, 'Don't be worried! Have faith in God and have faith in me. There are many rooms in my Father's house. I wouldn't tell you this, unless it was true. I am going there to prepare a place for each of you.'

JOHN 14:1–2

 Bible story link

The Bible describes death as passing through a valley. It paints a picture of a shepherd leading his sheep, providing everything that is needed: rest by streams of peaceful water, a guiding hand and true refreshment. Even when the path leads into a valley as dark as death, the shepherd is still there, offering protection and guidance. The journey eventually ends in a great feast at the table of the shepherd himself, where those who have followed the shepherd are treated as honoured guests. (Story synopsis based on Psalm 23.)

Saying goodbye to Poppy

'I don't want to go,' Sam moaned.

'Well, you've got to,' Mum said. 'You are coming to your grandfather's funeral and that is that. Now hurry up. You're not even dressed and we've got to go in ten minutes.'

Sam slouched upstairs and got out his football kit. He looked up to see Mum standing in the doorway of his bedroom.

'No,' she said, 'don't even think about it. Put on the new top I bought you yesterday. And don't forget to clean your teeth.'

'Postman's been,' Dad called out to no one in particular. 'Looks like another card.'

Sam heard the lid of the bin in the kitchen bang against the wall as the envelope was thrown away. He finished getting dressed and went to the bathroom. As he put his toothbrush back on the shelf, he heard Mum having a go at his big brother because his bedroom was a mess and he couldn't find a clean pair of socks.

Sam decided that today was going to be a bad day—the same as every day since last Saturday.

❖

The phone had rung first thing in the morning. A few minutes later, Sam had wandered into the kitchen to get his breakfast. He had a bit of a shock because Dad was sitting at the table crying his eyes out. Mum had her arm round his shoulders. She told him that Poppy had died.

Sam knew about dying because his pet gerbil had died last year. Mum had sat with him then while he had cried. She was doing the same now for Dad.

Sam was not sure what to do. He sort of wanted to cry, but wasn't sure if he should be really brave for Dad. So he went and stood by his dad and put his left hand on his shoulder. Mum looked up and whispered, 'We'll come and find you when we're ready. James is in the front room.'

'OK,' Sam whispered back and went to find his brother. He wanted to be with someone else. They had both loved their Poppy and now he was dead and they would never see him again.

Later that morning, Dad left to drive down to Nanny's. Sam went to play on the computer. Deep inside, he wanted to pretend Poppy was still alive.

When Dad came home that evening, he was very tired. He and Mum went in the front room together and closed the door.

'They want to talk without us,' James whispered. 'Let's go upstairs and get ready for bed.' It seemed important to help Mum and Dad, and that seemed the best thing to do.

Sam was just dropping off to sleep when Dad came into his bedroom. Sam opened his eyes and put his arms out for a hug.

'Poppy's not in pain any more,' Dad said, kneeling down beside the bed.

'I know,' Sam said. Then he asked, 'Is his body still in his bed where he died?'

'No, the funeral directors have taken it away.'

'Who?' Sam said. He had never heard of a 'funeral director'.

'They're the people who look after the body and organize the funeral.'

'Oh. Can you record the football for me tonight?'

Even as the words came out, Sam wondered if he had said the right thing. Mum had told him and James they were to be gentle with Dad. Was asking him to record football being gentle?

Sam need not have worried. 'You are wonderful,' Dad said as he gave him another hug. 'I've had a long, long day and you and James have got a special job to do this week.'

'What's that?' Sam asked.

'Just be yourselves,' Dad said and kissed the top of Sam's forehead. He stood up.

'Don't forget the football,' Sam called out as he walked towards the door.

'I won't,' Dad promised.

❖

And now it was five days later and they were in the car, driving to the funeral.

'What will happen at the service?' James asked as they reached the bottom of their road. 'It'll be dead boring,' Sam thought as an answer.

'We'll be in church,' Mum said. 'People will cry and get upset.'

'I'm not going to cry,' James interrupted. 'It's sissy to cry.'

'There's nothing wrong in crying,' Dad said, 'and it will be sad because we're saying "goodbye" to Poppy and giving thanks to God for his life.'

'Who'll be there?' James asked.

'All sorts of people—some from where Poppy used to work and the bowls club, and there will be some relatives you've never seen.'

'At least they can't say how much we've grown if they've

never seen us before,' he sighed.

'Where will Poppy's body be?' Sam asked, noisily turning over a page of the football magazine he was trying to read.

Mum tried not to sigh. She had been through this, and what would happen at the service, with both the boys already.

'His coffin with his body in will be at the front of the church,' she said.

Sam wrinkled up his nose. There had been a coffin on a television programme he had watched yesterday. A ghost had jumped out of it and scared people.

Mum seemed to have read his thoughts. 'The coffin will be closed,' she added, 'so you won't see Poppy's body.'

'And he won't become a ghost and jump out and say "hello" to us, will he?' Sam asked.

'No,' Mum replied.

'Dad saw Poppy's dead body last Saturday, though, didn't he?' James said.

'What did it look like?' Sam asked.

'As if he was asleep,' Dad said. 'They'd dressed him in his favourite suit.'

'Wasn't it creepy?' Sam wanted to know.

'No. Just very peaceful.'

They were quiet for a few seconds. Eventually, Sam asked Mum and Dad, 'You're not going to die, are you?'

'Well, one day,' Dad replied, 'but not for a long time yet, I hope.'

Sam tried to count how many white cars there were on the other side of the motorway. He had just reached 22 when Mum asked what they remembered most about Poppy.

'Playing chess and going to the park with him,' James said straight away.

'Seeing him wrapped up in a blanket and showing him my new game,' Sam added, thinking of the last time that he had seen him.

'Is that a nice memory?' Mum asked.

Sam nodded. It was like Poppy. He had been nice to be with even though he had sometimes told them off—for example, when Sam and James had walked all over the carpet in their muddy shoes.

'You know that after the service everyone will go to the hall along the road for something to eat and drink,' Mum said.

Sam sat up. No one had told him that bit before. Maybe church would not be too bad if there was food at the end of it. And after the food they would be going to the crematorium for another little service. Poppy's coffin would be left there to be burnt and the ashes buried in the ground. That was what happened at crematoriums. Sam knew because he had asked Mum. He also knew that some people's coffins were buried in the ground without being burnt.

'And don't forget about looking at the flowers,' Dad suddenly said. 'Everyone wants to talk about something afterwards, but they're not sure what to say,' he said, 'so they talk about the flowers.'

There would be some on top of the coffin and some laid out at the crematorium. They had got to look out for the yellow and blue ones because they were from Dad and Mum and James and Sam. Dad had ordered those because they were the same colours as Poppy's football team.

Eventually, they arrived at Nanny's. James and Sam went upstairs to keep out of the way. Quite a few people were coming and going to and from the house.

'Dad's wearing a suit,' James suddenly whispered and began giggling. Sam went over to the window where James was standing to have a look. Dad did not very often wear a suit. He looked a bit funny in it.

'Bet Mum's in that black dress she bought yesterday,' James said. 'She put it in the boot this morning.'

It was not long before Mum came upstairs for the boys. She

was now wearing... her black dress.

'Told you,' James whispered to Sam as they tiptoed downstairs behind her.

The hearse, with Poppy's coffin in it, had drawn up outside Nanny's house. People got into their own cars and followed as it drove, very slowly, to the church. When they arrived, four men lifted the coffin on to their shoulders. The vicar, who was going to take the service, came out to meet them.

'Where are the people from the bowls club?' Sam asked Mum as they walked up the church path.

'Inside the church already,' she whispered back. 'Only the family members come in behind the coffin.'

By now they had reached the church. There was a brief pause. When everyone was ready, the vicar started saying something in a loud voice and led the funeral procession into the building.

Sam was surprised at how light and warm the church was. Churches on television programmes were sometimes dark and spooky, but not this one. A man in a black suit gave him a printed sheet of paper.

'Thank you,' Sam whispered.

The man gave him a little smile. Sam did not look at the sheet of paper until he was sitting down next to Mum at the front of the church. It had Poppy's full name written at the top.

'I'm never going to see Poppy again,' Sam thought and suddenly felt very small. He hadn't really believed Poppy was dead until that moment, sitting there in this great big building with the coffin in front of him.

As the tears rolled down his cheeks, he buried his face in Mum's dress. It was safe there with her arm round him. The vicar was saying that a funeral was like opening a letter. If you thought of Poppy's body as the envelope, it was what was inside that was the important bit. Today they were going to think about the letter God had just received. They were going to think about Poppy and, in doing so, say 'goodbye' to him.

Sam wondered if God had a flip-top bin with a lid that banged on the wall if you flicked it too hard. He decided God probably did not.

The service lasted for about half an hour. There were readings and prayers and the vicar reminded them of some of the things Poppy had done when he was alive. After that first great wave of sadness, Sam was all right. He did not actually enjoy the funeral, but it was not too awful and he knew that everyone around him was feeling as sad as he was. In a funny sort of way, he found that a nice thought and was even glad that he had come.

When the service was over, they all followed the coffin out of church and waited while it was put back in the hearse to be taken to the crematorium. No one spoke much as they walked along the road to the hall.

Once they got inside, the adults did not seem to be hungry and stood around chatting. James and Sam did not mind because it meant they could help themselves to the food without being told not to pile their plates too high. Then they retreated into a corner and started to eat. They were the only children there. All their cousins were older and sat with the grown-ups.

After a while, Mum suggested the two of them went outside. That sounded like a good idea. They were getting tired of being quiet and good all the time. There was a park nearby and Mum said that they could let off steam there if they were very careful crossing the road and did not get too much mud on their clothes.

They had only been in the park for ten minutes when James announced that he was still hungry. 'And it's boring here,' he added. Sam agreed with him on both counts. He had hoped for something better than two swings and a seesaw that did not work properly.

'Shall we go back and see if there's any food left?' he suggested.

James nodded.

When they went back inside the hall, the first thing they noticed was the noise. People were chatting. There was even some laughter. Dad had taken his suit jacket off. Mum was digging into a sausage roll.

'Mum, why are people laughing?' Sam whispered. 'Aren't they sad about Poppy any more?'

Mum put her arm round him.

'We're all still sad,' she said, 'but everyone's starting to relax now.'

'Can we get some more food, then?' Sam asked.

'You and your tummy!' Mum sighed, then she added, 'You two are wonderful. You've really kept Dad and me going these last few days just because you've been yourselves. We'll still get sad, as you will be, about Poppy, but we've brought a lot of our sadness out in the open today and that's important.'

'Can I get some more food, then?' Sam asked again, pulling away from her.

Mum handed him her plate.

'Can you get me another sausage roll as well?' she added.

'All right,' Sam said, giving her a little grin.

Things children have said

'... grown-ups don't always think children feel things, but we do...'

'... you need to go to a funeral so you know what they're thinking and can all cry together...'

'... I wanted to go in the attic in my nanny's house because my grandad used to go up there. But I wasn't allowed to. I really miss him...'

'... my Mum was stressed. Not just a little bit, but really stressed. But I didn't answer her back or I'd have got in worse trouble...'

'... I'd get my little sister and we'd all get together for a family hug...'

Thinking time for children

Think about someone who has died. It could be someone famous or someone you actually knew. What do you remember about them? Do you miss them a lot or a little? Why? What did you do with them when they were alive? If you were to write them a letter, what would you tell them?

Thinking time activity

Make a card to give to someone who has lost a relative or friend. This could be someone in the news or someone you actually know. Think carefully about what you would want to write in the card and which picture you will draw on the front.

Prayer

Dear God, thank you for... and all the good times we shared together. Amen

Remembering

Story summary

Dermot's two best friends looked after him as he struggled against a long illness. A year after his death, his classmates remember him. As memories are carefully rewrapped, they realize that Dermot would want them to move on. The story looks at supporting others and the importance of facing up to loss before moving on.

RE concepts: Memorials and symbols

 Exploring the concept

Children's understanding

- ✪ Talk about what memories or artefacts children have of pets or people they have known who have died.
- ✪ Discuss how these are like symbols, representing the people or pets.

Religious overview

- ✪ Explore how faith communities mourn when one of their members dies.
- ✪ Discuss religious symbols that help people to remember and focus on their faith.

Christian viewpoint

Christians believe that remembering what Jesus did (especially how he died and came back to life again) helps their faith. The heart of Christian remembrance is in the breaking of bread and the sharing of wine at a service of Holy Communion, in which Jesus is remembered and the reality of his presence is celebrated. It is the belief in God's gift of eternal life through Jesus that gives cause for celebration even in the face of the loss of a loved one.

Do children agree with this viewpoint?

 Key Bible verses

You have turned my sorrow into joyful dancing. No longer am I sad and wearing sackcloth. I thank you from my heart, and I will never stop singing your praises, my Lord and my God.

PSALM 30:11–12

Bible story link

Just before Jesus died, he ate one last meal with his friends. Christians call this meal 'the Last Supper'. During the meal, Jesus took the bread and the wine, which were part of the 'remembering' story of the Jewish Passover feast, and used them to symbolize his death and resurrection. He said that the bread was his body and the wine his blood. The Christian service of Holy Communion re-enacts Jesus' words at the Last Supper. Communicants are given a small piece of bread and sip of wine in remembrance of Jesus' death and resurrection. (Story synopsis based on Matthew 26:26–29.)

Days in a week

It was a Monday when they first saw Dermot. The classroom door opened and the head teacher walked in, followed by a small boy wearing enormous glasses. Amir and Jermaine were asked to look after him.

Dermot loved school. It was a safe place where no one talked about hospital or tried to stick needles in him. Amir and Jermaine became his best mates. He joined in their games. He always played in goal. That way he did not get out of breath running round the playground.

It was on a Tuesday, several years later, when they realized how very ill Dermot was. He had not been to school for a while. Amir and Jermaine went to see him. They sat on his bed and played cards. Dermot cheated. Somehow it seemed important that he won, so they did not say anything. Jermaine looked at Dermot's eyes. They were sinking into his head. He was also having difficulty breathing.

Dermot only came to school one more time. Amir and Jermaine stayed in with him at playtime, and at lunchtime. They built a house out of Lego and played cards—for the last time. The head teacher joined them for a short while to make sure Dermot was coping all right.

In the afternoon they had a tables test. Dermot got two out of ten. No one minded. Later on, he began to cry. He said he was tired. He said his body was aching, all over.

'Do you want to go home?' the teacher asked.

Dermot nodded.

'Bye,' he whispered.

The door closed behind him.

It was on a Wednesday several weeks later that an ambulance took Dermot to hospital. Its siren wailed. Amir heard it as he walked home from school.

Dermot's life was draining away. Towards the end he smiled—a small flicker on a frozen face. He died at exactly half past six that evening.

The funeral was the following Thursday. Their teacher read a poem that Dermot had written a few months before. 'When I grow up...' it began. His parents cried. So did the teacher. So did everyone else. No one pretended to be brave. They were saying 'goodbye' to someone they loved.

A year passed—so slowly at first, then time gathered speed and the seasons changed and things moved on.

It was a Friday when they gathered in the school hall to remember Dermot. The girls sat on one side of the room, the boys on the other. It just happened that way. Just like Dermot's death had just 'happened'.

'We're here to remember Dermot,' the head teacher began.

No seats moved. No feet shuffled. Memories were being unwrapped. That DVD they had watched together, endless games on the PlayStation, his odd way of telling jokes, the way he pretended to dive for the ball when he was in goal. The fact that he never managed to learn his two times table.

'If I showed you these, who would you think of?' The head teacher took 'the' pack of playing cards from his pocket and held them up. Everyone laughed as the excitement and laughter Dermot could create from playing a simple game of cards danced in their brains. Those cards were like a symbol, a memorial to him.

'Dermot asked me to keep these safe,' the head teacher said. 'The last day he was in school, he gave them to me, and now I would like to give each of you one card as a reminder of a very special person.'

Slowly he handed the cards out. Amir got the two of clubs, Jermaine the eight of hearts. Then the head teacher read a story about a little girl who struggled to make a thousand paper birds. Death came for her before she finished her task. Yet those birds gave her a reason to live even as her body was growing tired.

Amir and Jermaine and all the others had played their part in giving Dermot a reason to live, too. They had been a safe place for him. They had loved him and cared for him and been his friend.

'Dear God, we thank you for Dermot's life,' the head teacher prayed. 'For all he meant to us.'

Amir did not want to pray. Jermaine did, though. He stared at the pattern the woodblocks made on the floor. He told God, yet again, how angry he was that Dermot had died, how unfair it was that they were all living now, and Dermot was not—that in a few minutes they would all stand up and walk out of this hall and be free to run around, and Dermot would not be with them—that their lives were ahead of them, and his was not.

But Dermot would not have wanted them to think like that. He would have wanted them to pause and remember him, yes. Then carefully wrap up their memories and keep them somewhere very safe as they moved on—as he had done. That's what Dermot would have wanted Amir, Jermaine and the others to do.

And that is what they did.

Things children have said

'... it's always sad when someone dies, even if you don't know them yourself, because everybody is known by somebody and you should feel sad for them...'

'... I felt upset and wanted to swap places with them, that God's unfair and nasty... and then I asked "why?"...'

'... everyone has to die sometime. It just depends how old they are and how well they knew the person who has died...'

'... some people don't care when someone dies. Like if they didn't know them...'

'... you can help someone by talking to them and listening to what they tell you...'

'... do little things to let them know you are thinking about them...'

Thinking time for children

If someone you know has died, think about them now. What is the best memory you have of them? Do you miss them as much now as when they first died? How would that person want you to remember them?

Thinking time activity

Think about someone (or a pet) you miss. It could be someone you know who has moved away. They do not have to have died. Now fold a piece of paper into four and draw or write about two different things you did with that person (or pet). Underneath, draw or write about two things you do now with someone else.

Prayer

Dear God, it's hard when people die, because we miss them. We wish they were alive again. It hurts inside. Amen

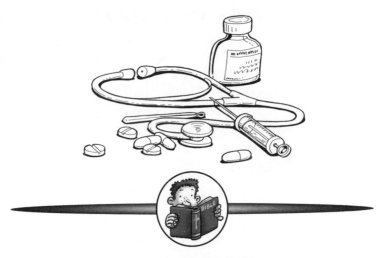

Serious illness

Story summary

Josie's mum is diagnosed with cancer and taken to hospital. Josie's dad explains what is happening and the visit to see her mum in hospital is told from Josie's point of view. The story encourages children to keep asking questions that are to be answered honestly.

RE concept: Suffering

 ## Exploring the concept

Children's understanding

- Talk about how children's families deal with illness.
- Discuss how knowing about something can take some of the fear away.

Religious overview

- Explore how faith communities care for people who are seriously ill.

Christian viewpoint

For some people, suffering is used as an argument to prove that God either does not exist or is vindictive. However, Christians believe that suffering can be seen as a challenge to help people become more reliant on God and, with his help, find out how good can eventually come out of an awful situation.

Do children agree with this viewpoint?

 ## Key Bible verses

Just thinking of my troubles and my lonely wandering makes me miserable. That's all I ever think about, and I am depressed. Then I remember something that fills me with hope. The Lord's kindness never fails! ... Deep in my heart I say, 'The Lord is all I need; I can depend on him!'

LAMENTATIONS 3:19–22a and 24

 ## Bible story link

The story of Job in the Old Testament is about a man who was very wealthy and had great faith in God. As a test to see whether he would stay faithful to God in the face of great distress, he lost his wealth, his children and, finally, his health. Through his struggles he came to a deeper understanding of God and faith in him. Job never understood why he had suffered but, even though he felt very bitter, he never rejected God or turned away from him. Job was convinced that some day God would rescue him. (Story synopsis based on Job 1:1–12 and 42:10–17.)

You're still my mum, even if you are ill

'It was kind of Joanna's mum to give you tea, wasn't it?' Dad said.

'Why is Mum in hospital?'

Dad took a deep breath. 'She's got cancer.'

There was something in Dad's voice that made Josie go cold all over. He took hold of her hand. 'Do you know what cancer is?'

'It's what Mr Kennedy had and he died.'

'Not everyone dies. The hospitals have loads of things they can do to get rid of it. Your body is made up of cells—millions and millions of them. Only Mum's got some cells that are nasty ones and she can't get rid of them. The doctors might do an operation or they might give her some drugs to try to stop the bad cells growing.'

'Is she going to die?'

'At the moment we don't know how far the cancer has spread,' he said slowly.

'Can't the doctors tell?'

'They've done some tests this afternoon. We'll get the results tomorrow.'

Josie wanted to cry and yet, at the same time, she also wanted to be brave and strong like Dad. Mums weren't supposed to get ill or go to hospital.

Dad sighed as he switched on the car engine. He had had a very long day. Mum had been feeling unwell for the last couple of weeks and had gone to see the doctor that morning. The doctor had sent her for a blood test and phoned just after eleven o'clock. Mum was to go straight to hospital for an emergency appointment. Dad met her there.

It had all happened so fast. Yesterday they were talking about going on holiday; today they were talking about cancer. Josie's voice broke into his thoughts.

'Can I get cancer?'

'It's not like a cold,' he said. 'It's one of those things. Some people get it. Others don't.' His voice trembled. Josie looked at him. The backs of her eyes were pricking and tears were making everything become blurry.

'I don't want her to die!' Josie sobbed.

'Neither do I,' Dad whispered. 'It's horrible to think that she might die—but for now we are hoping that she will be able to get well again. She is still trying to be cheerful. She says that even if there's lots of pain, there'll be some good that comes out of it—though at the moment I'm not sure how.'

The next day was Saturday. Dad was already downstairs when Josie got up.

'I phoned the hospital a few minutes ago,' he told her. 'I spoke to Felicity. She's one of the nurses looking after Mum. She said Mum had had a comfortable night and was looking forward to seeing us this morning.'

Josie smiled. It was only a little smile. She wanted the radio to be on and Mum sitting in her chair, flicking through the newspaper and talking to her.

'What's in the bag?' Josie asked, as she and Dad got ready to leave half an hour later.

'A clean nightie, a couple of magazines and a card from Joanna's mum... oh, and can you get the towel and that new tube of toothpaste I put at the bottom of the stairs? They can go in, too.'

Josie nodded. She was feeling a bit nervous. She had never been in a hospital before, apart from when she was born—and she could not remember much about that.

Josie slipped her hand into her dad's as they walked towards the hospital building. Bleak, black-rimmed windows were sandwiched between layers of concrete.

'Mum's up on the fourth floor above that lamp-post,' Dad said, pointing straight ahead of them.

'Oh!' Josie said. She was trying to read the sign attached to the lamp-post. The words were too long and she didn't know what they meant.

'What do those words say?' she asked Dad.

'Haematology and oncology,' Dad said.

Josie screwed up her nose.

'Haematology is blood and oncology is cancer.'

'Why can't they just call it blood and cancer?'

'That would be too easy and nothing is easy at the moment.'

Josie wanted to go in the lift because she liked pressing the buttons, but Dad said the stairs would be quicker. Normally, she would have made a fuss and they would have gone in the lift, but not today.

There were more long words at the top of the stairs.

'Chemotherapy. Radiotherapy,' Dad read.

'Where's speech therapy?' One of Josie's friends had been for that when they were in Year 2 at school.

'Chemotherapy and radiotherapy are both ways of attacking the nasty cancer cells,' Dad said. 'You won't find speech therapy up here. That's for helping you speak more clearly.'

'Oh.'

Josie suddenly felt very small, surrounded by all these

long words that she had never heard of before, and strange smells and busy-looking people pushing trolleys down long corridors.

'Because of the risk of infection, please do not bring any flowers into the ward,' Josie read. 'Are we allowed to take in the toothpaste and towel?'

Dad nodded.

They were passing a machine that sold canned drinks and chocolate bars. 'Remember where this machine is,' Dad said. 'You can treat yourself to something from it later on.'

He held the huge wooden door open for her. It had a metal strip running across it halfway down.

'That strip's to protect the door when they wheel trolleys in and out,' Dad said. He was trying to explain everything. Josie thought he was going a bit over the top, but did not say so. Instead, she nodded again and reached up for his hand. It was strong and smooth and made her feel a little bit better until Dad let go.

'Need to wash our hands with this spray now,' he said, reaching towards a plastic tube with a spray pump on top.

'Antibacterial handwash,' Josie read.

'Stops us taking bugs into the ward,' said Dad.

They went down another corridor with lots of doors in it. Some of them were open. Josie peeped inside. A loo. A little kitchen and some sinks. An elderly man with a tube up his nose. A desk at which a nurse was sitting on a chair, surrounded by little trolleys, folders and computers. The nurse stood up and smiled at Dad. Josie read her name badge. 'Felicity Summers.'

'Hello,' Felicity said. 'You must be Josie. Your mum told me all about you this morning.'

Josie smiled.

'Is my mummy getting better?' she asked.

'We'll do our very best,' Felicity smiled, then she spoke to

Dad in an adult tone. 'You know where she is, don't you?'

Mum was sitting up in bed, reading the newspaper, but all Josie saw was the bleeping machine next to Mum's bed. There was a tube coming from it. Josie's eyes followed that tube to the place where it went into the back of Mum's hand.

Josie didn't like that machine. It was part of Mum being ill. It was part of Mum being in hospital. It made her feel small again and stopped her being brave and grown-up and...

'Josie,' Dad said, 'are you coming to give Mum a hug?'

Josie looked beyond the machine to Mum's smiling face.

'Come round this side,' Mum said, patting the bed with her other hand, 'then the machine won't get in the way. It's really nice to see you.'

They talked about what Josie had done at school the day before and what they'd had for breakfast. Mum needed help filling in the order form for her meal that evening. Josie ticked beef and onion pie with mashed potatoes and a chocolate éclair for pudding.

'I shall look forward to that all day,' Mum said.

Then Felicity came to check Mum's temperature and blood pressure.

'That's fine,' she smiled and wrote in the red file hanging on a piece of string from the bottom of the bed, next to where Mum's feet were making a little hill under the bedcovers. 'The doctors will be really pleased with that.'

'Are you getting better?' Josie asked. 'Will you be home soon?'

'We'll have to wait and see what the doctors say,' Mum sighed.

Dad smiled. Mum smiled. Josie smiled, too. Maybe the doctors would be so pleased with Mum that she could come home with them.

A few minutes later, three people in white coats appeared at the bottom of the bed. One of them picked up the red file that Felicity had written in.

'Hello, Doctor Simpson,' Mum said.

'Josie,' Dad whispered, 'do you fancy getting some cans of drink and chocolate bars out of that machine I showed you?'

Josie looked at all the adults standing round the bed. They all smiled at her, but she knew they wanted her to leave. This was one of those times when adults talk to each other and do not want children around.

'Are you Josie?' one of them asked.

Josie nodded.

'How old are you?'

'Nine.'

'I've got a daughter who's ten. She's in Year 5.'

'I'm in Year 5 as well.'

'So you must have your birthday soon.'

'Next month,' Josie said, nodding. Dad was taking some money out of his pocket.

'There you go,' he said. She must be a good girl. She stood up.

'Thanks, love,' Dad said. 'See you in a few minutes.'

Josie went back to the doors with metal strips to the drink and snack machine. Cans of orangeade clattered into the black opening at the bottom of the machine. She bought a chocolate bar as well.

The elderly man still had the tube up his nose. She looked in his room to check as she walked back.

'Hello,' Felicity said from behind her desk. 'The doctors are still with your mum. Do you want to sit by me for a few minutes until they've finished?'

She pulled a chair over for Josie to sit on. Before long, Josie knew that Felicity supported Liverpool, had three big brothers and used to have a hamster called Tickle.

'Is my mummy's hair going to fall out?' Josie suddenly asked. It was nothing to do with football or hamsters, but that did not matter. 'That man in the room back there, the one with the tube up his nose, he's got no hair. And Mr Kennedy lost all his as well. Will Mum?'

'Hopefully not,' Felicity answered. 'It depends whether she has to have chemotherapy or not, and what sort she has.'

'Oh.'

They sat in silence for a moment, then Josie asked in a very small voice, 'Is my mummy going to die?'

Felicity looked straight at Josie. She was going to be honest. There was no point in not being.

'We don't know how far the cancer's spread,' she said. 'We've got to do some more tests. Then we'll have a better idea.'

'If she does die, will she go to heaven?'

Felicity thought about that one for a moment.

'That depends on what she believes,' she answered.

'What's heaven like?'

'I've only ever heard that it's good,' Felicity answered. Then she added, 'You know what?'

'What?'

'You're brilliant because you keep asking questions. I bet you're one of those people who keep asking questions until you're happy with the answers, aren't you?'

Josie moved her head up and down in a slow nod. She liked Felicity.

A few minutes later, three white coats swept down the corridor.

'Did you get your orangeade?' Dr Simpson asked.

Josie nodded. 'And a bar of chocolate,' she said.

'Are you OK with Felicity for a bit longer? Your dad will come and find you in a minute or two.'

'That's fine,' Felicity said and smiled, 'even if she does support Manchester United.'

It wasn't long before Dad appeared.

'See you later,' Felicity said as Josie slipped off her chair and went to him.

Mum and Dad had both been crying. Josie could tell because their eyes were red.

Mum was having an operation on Tuesday with a course of chemotherapy afterwards.

'I just can't believe this is happening,' Josie heard Dad say. He told her the name of the type of cancer Mum had. Three very long and difficult words that she couldn't remember.

'Oh,' she whispered.

She had had enough. She wanted to go home.

With Dad.

And Mum.

Things children have said

'... children always want to know the truth about what is happening...'

'... you always want to know if someone is going to be all right, only you don't always know, do you?...'

'... I found these long words on Saturday when I went to hospital to see my grandad: morphine, medication, stethoscope, operation, transplant, chemotherapy, injection, radiotherapy, consultant, paediatrics, accident and emergency. I don't know what half of them mean. He had tubes in him, but they didn't scare me because they were there to help him...'

'... cancer can kill you and if you have it, it makes lumps come under your skin...'

'... you get it from smoking...'

'... when you first get cancer it's a bit of a shock...'

'... you *lose* your hair with it...'

'... my grandma had *breast* cancer, but she's OK now...'

'... Dad would have to do more jobs and that would make him more tired and he'd probably get really cross with Josie sometimes, but he wouldn't really mean to...'

'... just her presence around the house. She wouldn't *be* there, would she? Only there would *be* loads of things to keep making you think about her...'

'... she couldn't tuck Josie up in bed at night. Children need their mum...'

'... not being there to help with the homework and not being involved in decisions...'

'... Josie would be feeling sad, afraid, lonely, uncomfortable, nervous, frightened, ill herself, weird, couldn't concentrate, wanting Mum to come home, confused, a rumbling feeling inside her tummy...'

'... adults need time to talk on their own...'

'... they want to decide what they are going to tell Josie. They don't always tell children everything. Sometimes that's stupid, but other times that is the right thing to do. That's what they did with us when Gran was ill...'

'... I'd want to buy her a present to make her get better...'

'... the doctor might need to do something to Mum that they wouldn't want Josie to see...'

'... I'd want to know if she would still be the same mum like she used to be...'

Thinking time for children

If you know someone who is very ill, how do you feel about them? Do you have someone you can talk to about them? Is there something you can do to show them how special they are to you?

Thinking time activity

Design a card to send to someone who is very ill. Think carefully about what you would want to write inside it. Write a poem to tell someone how special they are to you. Maybe you could write an acrostic poem so that the person's name is spelt if you read down the first letter of each line.

Prayer

Dear God, I'm thinking of................. I don't know why they are ill. Please help the doctors and nurses to know how to look after them. Amen

Learning
to behave
responsibly

Story summary

Joanna and Rachel are on holiday in Spain with Joanna's parents. Forbidden to jump off the jetty into the sea, they make a pact to do just that in the dark on the last night. The fatal accident that follows leads Joanna to reflect on how actions have consequences. The story demonstrates an extreme consequence of behaving irresponsibly.

RE concept: Regret

 Exploring the concept

Children's understanding
- Talk about things children have done that they have later regretted.
- Discuss the consequences of both responsible and irresponsible behaviour.
- Explore how regret can be turned into a positive outcome or feeling.

Religious overview
- Discuss how different religions give guidance for behaving responsibly.

Christian viewpoint
Christians believe that the Bible gives them all the guidance they need to live a good and honest life. For Christians, the Ten Commandments are the basis on which to build a lifestyle of respect: for others, for themselves and for God. Christians believe that Jesus is the perfect role model for these ten 'best ways' to live and he demonstrated their wisdom in everything he said and did.

Do children agree with this viewpoint?

 Key Bible verses

Respect your father and your mother... Do not murder... Do not steal. Do not tell lies about others. Do not want to take anything that belongs to someone else.

EXODUS 20:12–13 and 15–17

Bible story link

One day, when he was travelling through the town of Jericho, Jesus met a man named Zacchaeus, who was very rich. Zacchaeus collected taxes for the Romans. Tax collectors often cheated people out of their money and, for this reason, were hated by ordinary people. Jesus invited himself to Zacchaeus' house and spent time with him. As a result of this meeting, Zacchaeus' life was transformed and he regretted the way he had cheated and robbed people in order to line his own pockets. Consequently, he promised to give half his property to the poor and to pay back four times as much to everyone he had ever cheated. (Story synopsis based on Luke 19:1–10.)

The jetty

One of the first things Mum told the two girls when the family arrived at the hotel was not to jump into the sea from the end of the jetty.

'The water is very deep and there are strong currents,' she said, 'and we don't want either of you being swept out to sea, do we?'

Joanna looked enviously at the older boys screaming and laughing as they hurtled along the jetty before throwing themselves off the end into the sea. There were weathered stone steps cut into the concrete wall to help them get out of the water before they ran down the jetty again. It looked such fun and she and Rachel were both good enough swimmers, even if Mum didn't think so.

That night the two girls made up their minds.

'Your mum and dad don't have to know,' Rachel said. 'We'll

sneak out of the apartment at night when they're in the bar and do it. Just once, that'll be enough.'

'But you're not supposed to go swimming in the sea when it's dark. There's a sign downstairs.'

'So? If we're supposed *not* to be jumping off the jetty, *nor* swimming in the dark, it'll be a double dare: double danger, double excitement and double everything! And let's do it on the last night. Your parents can't punish us then if they do find out.'

'Done!'

They had a brilliant holiday. The sun was hot, the ice creams were cold, the trips to the volcano and the old castle were great and, on Friday evening, there was a concert in the hotel bar.

'We'd rather stay in our apartment on our own,' Joanna told her mum.

'Are you sure?' Her mother looked surprised. The girls had moaned about going to bed before midnight every other night.

'We're dead tired. And we've got to get up early for the plane.'

Mum frowned. She sensed they were up to something.

'I can trust you, can't I?'

'Of course you can.'

Of course she could. They had been so sensible during the week.

❖

Mum and Dad only saw the first half of the concert. A shivering, sobbing Joanna appeared during the interval and the police patrol boat found Rachel's body half an hour later.

'Why did you do it?' Mum asked for the umpteenth time. They were back in their apartment now. The concert had been abandoned and Rachel's parents were being contacted in England.

'Why?' her mother asked again. But Joanna couldn't say.

She wanted to hide, to pretend it hadn't happened, to go to sleep and wake up and find it was all a bad dream.

'Why couldn't it have been you who drowned?' her mother suddenly shouted at her.

'Sandra!' Joanna's father gasped. 'How could you say that?'

'Because it was such a stupid thing to do! I told them not to and they ignored me. If they hadn't, Rachel would still be alive and...'

Then Mum had her arms round Joanna, hugging her, crying again.

'I didn't mean it,' she sobbed.

'People say things they don't mean when they're upset,' her father added, feeling angry, upset, guilty and nervous all at the same time.

Joanna still said nothing. Rachel had bought her a present — a bag covered with sequins. It was on her bed, so she couldn't have drowned. She'd walk through the door in a moment and they could all go to sleep. Only she didn't. She really had gone; really had drowned. The two of them had taken a risk and it had gone wrong. Wishing they hadn't would never bring Rachel back again.

Things were happening around Joanna. She watched without taking part. A policewoman was saying she would be back tomorrow to interview them all again. Her father was crying while he was talking on the phone. Other people came into the room and then went back out again. The manager of the hotel was scratching his head and talking to a policeman in Spanish. A doctor was telling her to swallow some medicine to help her sleep.

If only she and Rachel had gone to the concert, none of this would have happened. And what would everyone say at school? They'd all know about it. The newspaper reporters had already been to the hotel reception asking to speak to her. They were English reporters. Mum had said so.

She was a good girl, really. It had just been tonight when she hadn't been. They had wanted to be like the older boys who had been jumping off the jetty. Only Rachel hadn't been able to grasp the weathered steps, and her hands had waved frantically as the current dragged her further and further away into the darkness. Joanna had just stood there, shouting helplessly at her friend as she disappeared.

'I'm sorry,' she whispered. And she really was.

Things children have said

'... it's OK to cry when someone dies. My dad cried at my granny's funeral...'

'... you have to think of what might happen every time you do something...'

'... people say things they regret saying afterwards. Things like they wish they had never been born, hurtful things they don't mean, and they might swear when they don't usually...'

'... it'll be hard at school. Rachel's other friends might be horrible to her...'

'... she'll feel ill and cry a lot. Joanna has lost her best friend and is sorry. She might get depressed and blame herself...'

'... nothing will make it better for her. She has to live with what happened...'

Thinking time for children

What is the hardest thing about being responsible? Think of all the things you do. Which have risks attached and which don't? What do you do about keeping yourself safe when you do something? What would happen if you never took any risks at all?

Thinking time activity

Think of five things you enjoy doing. Which has the most risk attached? Put the five things in order, with the one carrying the most risk at the top. How do you make sure you are safe? Write down some rules to keep yourself safe.

Prayer

Dear God, be with those who are having to deal with the consequences of their actions today. Amen

Looking after living things

Story summary

Jasmine and Paul help their mum to look after their neighbour's plants and pet cat while she is on holiday. During the week, the cyclamen is over-watered and the cat has to visit the vet. The story covers issues related to caring for our world.

RE concept: Sustaining the natural world

 Exploring the concept

Children's understanding

- ☯ Talk about how children can look after the world they live in by recycling and being careful with resources.
- ☯ Explore what could be done to preserve the earth's resources better.
- ☯ Discuss how rich nations could help poorer nations by distributing resources more fairly.

Religious overview

- ☯ Discuss how different religions view the world.

Christian viewpoint

Christians believe that when God made the world, he gave human beings the responsibility of caring for his creation. Therefore, people have stewardship of all living things and should care for them properly.

Do children agree with this viewpoint?

 Key Bible verses

God created humans to be like himself; he made men and women. God gave them his blessing and said: 'Have a lot of children! Fill the earth with people and bring it under your control. Rule over the fish in the sea, the birds in the sky, and every animal on the earth.'

GENESIS 1:27–28

As the people in the world began to grow in number, the Bible tells us they started to behave in ways which made God very sorry that he had created human beings in the first place.

God decided to start again. He chose a man who had great faith in God. Noah and his wife loved God and lived good lives that were pleasing to him. God told Noah to build an ark (a large boat), even though Noah lived miles from the sea. When the ark was completed, Noah filled it with a pair of every species of animal and bird. When the ark was full and the door was shut, it started to rain. It rained for forty days and forty nights and at the end of that time the world was completely covered with water.

After the flood had subsided, the animals disembarked and Noah said 'thank you' to God for keeping them all safe. In response, God made a promise never to destroy the world by flood again. The symbol of God's promise was a rainbow. As long as the world remains, God promises that there will be planting and harvest, cold and heat, summer and winter, day and night. (Story synopsis based on Genesis 7:1—9:17.)

Alfie, the cyclamen and Grandad

Whenever Mrs Stibbs went on holiday, Jasmine's and Paul's mum looked after her plants and fed the cat.

'As always, Alfie will need a bit of loving,' Mrs Stibbs said when she left the key at their house the day before she headed for Spain. 'And don't forget, the umbrella plant has to be covered in water all the time. It's the tall one in the porch with sticky-up leaves.'

'Don't you worry,' Mum said. 'You just go and have a

fantastic time. Enjoy all that sunshine and food—and sitting with your feet up.'

Mrs Stibbs left on Saturday morning, just as Jasmine and Paul were off to see Grandad, who lived on the other side of town. They waved as the taxi pulled away. Grandad had a cat called Malcolm, a canary called George, a goldfish called Winston and a tin full of chocolate biscuits, which was half empty by the time Jasmine and Paul returned home at six o'clock that evening. Alfie was waiting for them, sitting by their front door, purring.

'He knows we're looking after him,' Mum laughed. 'Let's go and feed him now.'

Mrs Stibbs' house key was on a keyring with a monkey dangling from it. Mum unlocked the porch door first, then the front door. Meanwhile, Alfie raced round the side of the house and dived through the cat flap in the back door. He sat in the hall waiting for them and followed Mum into the kitchen, his tail held high in the air. He watched carefully as Mum took a half-finished can of cat food out of the fridge. Then he sprang on to the work surface and tried to stick his nose in the can while Mum spooned the food into his blue plastic dish.

'You're a very funny little black cat,' she told him, 'with sticking-out ears and a great fat hungry tummy.' Alfie purred even louder.

Mum lowered the dish on to the mat by the kitchen door. The cat followed it and crouched low, sticking his face into the food and making munching noises.

Sunday came and went, and on Monday the plants also needed checking.

'They'll need a very little bit of water,' Mum told Jasmine as she filled up the watering can at the sink. 'Except the umbrella plant—that will need to be covered.'

Jasmine carefully carried the can to the front room. On the windowsill was a plant, a beautiful cyclamen with deep red flowers that looked like fairies' wings. The soil was moist but not wet, so Jasmine lifted the watering can and in two seconds the soil round the cyclamen was covered with water.

'That's better,' she whispered. 'I'll look after you, little plant.' Then she headed for the porch. The umbrella plant pot also needed topping up. In all, she found six plants downstairs and one upstairs (in the bathroom) and carefully watered them all. By the time she had finished, Mum and Paul had fed Alfie, put the post on the kitchen table and checked all the rooms in the house. Everything was fine.

'Well done!' Mum said as she once more locked the front door and then the porch door.

It was Wednesday morning when they noticed that Alfie was limping. It seemed to be his back right paw that was causing him trouble.

'Let me have a look, little one,' Mum said gently, but Alfie had no intention of letting anyone near his paw and spat and hissed at her.

'OK, then,' Mum said, backing off. 'I've got to take Jasmine and Paul to school. Then I'll come back and have another look at you.'

But, half an hour later, Alfie still wouldn't let Mum have a look at his back paw. She decided to leave him until the evening and see if he was better then.

That evening, as they walked past Mrs Stibbs' front window, Mum noticed the beautiful red fairy flowers of the cyclamen. They weren't standing tall any more. Instead, they were drooping sadly over the sides of the pot.

'I wonder what's happened to that plant,' she said.

'I've been watering it, Mum,' Jasmine said.

'Oh,' Mum said. 'How much water?'

'Like the umbrella plant.'

'Uh-oh!' Mum said. 'My fault—I should have told you. Cyclamens like a bit of water poured down the side of their pot, never ever over the top of them. That's the quickest way to kill them. Right, we'll pour all the water off and leave the pot in the sink to drain. Can you carry it to the kitchen for me? Now where's the cat? I'm more worried about him than I am about the plant.'

Alfie was nowhere to be seen. Neither had he finished his breakfast. Half of it was still in his plastic bowl. Paul found him lying on Mrs Stibbs' bed. His eyes were half-shut and he didn't stretch and yawn and purr in the way he usually did.

'I think you need to go to the vet,' Mum sighed, stroking Alfie's head. 'You're not very well, are you?'

'How will we get him there?' Paul asked.

'Mrs Stibbs must have a travelling box, but I don't know where it is,' Mum said. 'We'll have to borrow Malcolm's from Grandad.'

So they locked Mrs Stibbs' house up and drove over to see Grandad, who thought it was great having an extra visit from them. He wanted to know all about Alfie and gave Paul and Jasmine a chocolate biscuit each when Mum wasn't looking.

'You will phone and let me know what happens, won't you?' he said as they left.

'We will,' Mum promised.

The vet explained that Alfie had an infection in his back paw. He prescribed some antibiotics. That should sort Alfie out in a day or two. Mum thought about letting Alfie sleep in their kitchen that night but, in the end, decided he would be better in his own house.

By the next evening, Alfie was feeling much better and even purred when they came to greet him. Paul sat next to him and stroked his long black fur.

'You're going to be all right now,' he told him, then screeched in pain, snatching his hand away from Alfie's sharp claws.

'Ow! Mum, the cat just scratched me and I'm bleeding.'

'Maybe he just wants to be left in peace,' Mum suggested. 'We'll clean the scratch and put a plaster on it when we get home. Let me just check the cyclamen.'

'Is it going to be all right?' Jasmine asked.

'I think so,' Mum said. 'We spotted it just in time. You have to remember, if it's alive it needs looking after in its own special way.'

'Am I alive?' Jasmine said, staying absolutely still. Mum looked at her doubtfully, then tickled her. Jasmine laughed.

'I think you probably are, and you need lots of care to keep you healthy.'

Things children have said

'... everyone needs caring for and looking after, even if they think they're all right...'

'... everyone needs love...'

'... keeping alive is hard work...'

'... you need light and air and food. My cat eats Whiskas and won't touch that cheap stuff Mum gets sometimes. She gets really cross with him and tries to hide it by mixing them up, but he still won't touch it...'

'... you also need oxygen and somewhere to live...'

'... and love. My mum talks to her plants when she waters them and we all laugh at her. She says it's her way of showing them she loves them. I think she's nuts...'

'... elderly people need looking after because of diseases and they get lonely...'

'... I wish my grandparents lived nearer. They live in London and we never see them. Shireen sees hers, all the time...'

Thinking time for children

Think of three things you've done to help a person, an animal or a plant stay alive. What other things could you do? Who is keeping you alive? What can we do to help keep planet earth healthy?

Thinking time activity

Draw two things you can think of at home, two at school, two in your local area and two in the world (eight things altogether) that need looking after in a special way.

Prayer

Dear God, anything that is alive is special and needs looking after if it is to grow and stay healthy. Sometimes it's easy to do that. Sometimes it's hard. Help us to keep going when it seems difficult. Thank you for our families and pets. Amen

Community life

Racial issues

Story summary

Siguna was born with green skin. As he is about to go to a new school, his mother paints him a light brown colour, but his new classmates find out his secret and are unkind to him. His new teacher gives blue and red bands to the children and treats them according to their band colour to teach them a lesson. The story raises issues about acceptance of others' backgrounds, experiences and skin colour.

RE concept: Respect for other people

 ## Exploring the concept

Children's understanding
- ✪ Talk about things that make people different.
- ✪ Discuss how everyone should be respected and treated equally regardless of their appearance or background.

Religious overview
- ✪ Explore how respect should be shown for a person's religion.

Christian viewpoint
Christians believe that prejudice of any kind goes against the will of God and is unacceptable. Throughout his life, Jesus reached out to those who were rejected and despised in society—a fact that often got him into trouble with the religious leaders of his day. In his letter to the Christians who lived in the region of Galatia (in central Asia Minor), the apostle Paul wrote, 'Faith in Christ Jesus is what makes each of you equal with each other, whether you are a Jew or a Greek, a slave or a free person, a man or a woman' (Galatians 3:28).

Do children agree with this viewpoint?

 ## Key Bible verse

The Lord told him, '… People judge others by what they look like, but I judge people by what is in their hearts.'
1 SAMUEL 16:7

Bible story link

In response to the question, 'Who are my neighbours?', Jesus told a story about a man who was travelling from the city of Jerusalem to the town of Jericho. On the way, the man was attacked by robbers. Three people came along after the attack. The first was a priest who, when he saw the man lying half-dead by the side of the road, hurried by on the other side. The second was a temple worker who, when he saw that the man had been beaten up, also walked by on the other side. Finally, a man from Samaria came upon the stricken man. Samaria was an area to the north of Judea, where customs were different from those in Jerusalem. The Samaritans were despised by the Jewish people and treated with contempt. However, this man was the only person who stopped to help the injured man.

The story is an illustration of Jesus' teaching that we should respect all people, regardless of their origins, beliefs and values. (Story synopsis based on Luke 10:25–37.)

We're all different

'I've put my tooth under the pillow,' Siguna said. 'Are you sure the tooth fairy will be able to find me?'

'Of course she will,' Mither replied. 'Now, try to get some sleep. You've got a busy day ahead of you.'

She bent over and gave him a kiss. 'I hope everything's all right tomorrow,' she thought.

Siguna closed his eyes. The next thing he knew, sunlight was streaming through the curtains and it was morning. He slid his hand under his pillow. The tooth fairy had been. Brilliant!

'I shall buy some sweets with this tonight,' he whispered, clutching a silver coin in his hand, 'to give to my new friends.'

He got out of bed and went to find Mither. They had breakfast together and then Mither took out some face paints and painted Siguna's face and hands a light brown colour. The brush tickled and he began giggling.

'You look like you've been in the sun now,' Mither laughed when she had finished. 'We'll just do this for a couple of days, until everyone at school gets used to you.'

Siguna held Mither's hand very tightly as they walked across the playground.

'They're all looking at me,' he whispered.

'They're probably thinking how nice it's going to be to get to know you,' Mither whispered back.

'Are they?' Siguna asked in an even quieter whisper.

Mither and Siguna had a chat with the head teacher before he was taken across to his new classroom. Mrs Jennings' class were doing quiet reading. She looked up and smiled as he came through the door. Siguna liked her straight away. She had long brown hair and bright red nail varnish on her fingernails.

Mrs Jennings took Siguna to a table where several children looked over the tops of their books and grinned at him.

'Jess and Sam will look after you today,' she said kindly. 'There's your chair and you've got a drawer under the table. I've done a label with your name on already. We're just about to get ready for PE.'

Siguna went cold all over. Not PE. Anything but PE. Not on the first lesson of the first day in a new place.

It was not that he was useless at PE. Siguna loved it, and was great at doing handstands and climbing ropes and playing football. It was just that he did not, under any circumstance whatsoever, want to take his jumper off. Not today, anyway.

'Don't worry if you haven't got anything to change into,'

Mrs Jennings said. 'We can go to lost property and find you something to wear. In fact, I think we've got something in the cupboard already.'

Siguna looked at the T-shirt and shorts he had been given. He glanced over his shoulder to see if anyone was watching. They all seemed to be busy talking to each other and getting changed themselves, so he lifted his jumper up really fast, pulled it over his head and reached out for the T-shirt, struggling to get it on as quickly as he could.

Too slow!

'That new boy's got green skin!' someone gasped.

There was laughing and giggling behind him as other children crowded round to have a look. Siguna felt someone touch his back.

'Bet he smells,' someone whispered. 'Fancy having green skin.' Even Sam and Jess, who had been asked to look after him, joined in the staring and whispering. Siguna wished he were back home.

'Does it matter?' he wanted to shout out. 'I'm still a person and I have feelings and I hurt when you stare at me and whisper about me and touch my back. I was born with green skin and I can't change that and... and...'

But he did not even open his mouth. He was different. He hated being different, but he was and always would be. He simply pulled the T-shirt down and sat in his seat, looking at the table. The tear that rolled down his cheek washed a line through the face paint, showing more green skin underneath. He wiped the tear away with the back of his hand and the paint on his hand became smudged as well as that on his face.

Mrs Jennings came over and put her arm round him.

'I can't believe what's just happened,' she said.

'I want to go home,' Siguna whispered. 'Please let me.'

'You've got to stick it out,' Mrs Jennings said. 'But I'm going to help you, because I think this lot have been horrible and I'm ashamed of them.'

She did not give Siguna a chance to answer before she stood up.

'Right. Finish changing in silence and then line up.' She spat the words out. Her voice was not kind or friendly any more, but harsh and angry. 'Maybe by the end of this PE lesson you'll all have learned something important,' she barked.

They walked across to the hall in silence. Siguna held Mrs Jennings' hand and stayed by her as everyone got out the large PE apparatus. There was a huge climbing frame and ropes and rope ladders and plastic tunnels to climb through—much more than there had been at Siguna's last school.

In one corner, Mrs Jennings told some of the children to put out four large mats. Then she gave out coloured bands. Five were blue, all the others were red. The children were then allowed on the apparatus. They could go anywhere they wanted to.

'Do you want to go on the apparatus?' Mrs Jennings asked Siguna.

'No,' he whispered and shook his head. He felt safe by the teacher. She gave him a sad, gentle smile.

'All children with red bands, sit on the mats, please,' she suddenly announced. 'Blue bands, stay on the apparatus.'

Blue bands, of course, thought this was wonderful. They climbed and swung on the ropes while the others had to watch.

'What about us?' one of the children on the mats called out.

'You're wearing red bands, so you don't count,' she snapped and then ignored them.

The five blue-band children began pulling faces and laughing at those sitting on the mats.

'How do we become blues?' someone asked.

'You can't,' Mrs Jennings said. 'Once you're a red, you're always a red and that's that. Now be quiet.'

'Why are you being nice to them and not us?' someone else asked a few minutes later.

'I'm just letting you know how Siguna must have felt this morning,' Mrs Jennings said in a cold voice.

'It's not fair them getting all the goes on the apparatus,' someone else piped up.

'I have asked you to be quiet,' Mrs Jennings snapped. 'What you say or think does not bother me in the least. You should have been born a blue.'

There was silence for several minutes, apart from the noise of five children climbing on the apparatus. Then the blue bands were asked to join the red ones on the mats.

'It's not very nice when some people are treated differently, is it?' Mrs Jennings said to them all. 'But that is how you treated Siguna this morning. You laughed at him and talked about him behind his back. I was appalled by the way you behaved. It doesn't matter what colour anyone's skin is, or where they come from, or what language they speak, they are still the same as you and they hurt inside when you are nasty to them. Every single one of you is special and loved just because you are you.'

The children stared at her. She did not get angry very often.

'I think,' Mrs Jennings carried on, 'we'll start this lesson again. In a minute you can take your bands off. Then anyone with freckles can go on the climbing frame, and those who normally wear glasses can use the rope ladders...'

It was then that Siguna heard something that made his hair stand on end with happiness.

'What do you want?' Mrs Jennings asked the boy who had put his hand up.

'Can Siguna be in my group?' he said.

'That would be lovely,' Mrs Jennings said and smiled. 'But which group will it be? We've had freckles and glasses.'

'What about those with a front tooth missing?' someone

suggested and everyone, including Siguna, laughed out loud.

'Brilliant,' their teacher said, 'and that group can go and work where the benches and hoops are.'

Things children have said

'... people that laugh at you are sad themselves...'

'... it doesn't matter what you look like on the outside. You could have freckles or spots or anything. It's what you're like inside that's important. That's what I think, anyway...'

'... people who are nasty to other people are horrible themselves...'

'... you mustn't listen if someone says something you don't like. You must ignore them, then they go away. Only they don't always. Then you have to tell a grown-up, like a teacher or a dinner lady or your mum or dad, and they have to do something about it. If they don't they're letting you down...'

'... when I meet someone for the first time, I always look at how friendly they look, if they are smiling and if their hands have got little wrinkles on them like my gran has...'

'... I do look at the colour of their skin but I don't mind what it is...'

Thinking time for children

Has anyone ever done anything nasty to you because you were different from them? What did it feel like? Are you still upset about it? How can you try to stop it happening again? Have you ever been nasty to someone? What did it feel like? Did you like it when they got upset? Would you upset them again? Why?

Thinking time activity

Make up a modern-day version of the parable of the good Samaritan.

Prayer

Dear God, we're all different and that is how you made us. Sometimes people are nasty, though, and laugh and say horrible things. Please help me to know what to do if that happens again. Amen

Gender issues

Story summary

A group of children are raising money for charity by visiting as many London underground stations as possible in one day. Along with their adult helpers, the children split into two groups: boys and girls. The story confronts gender stereotypes through the comments the children make about the other team.

RE concept: Equality

 Exploring the concept

Children's understanding

- ☯ Talk about the perceptions children have of the other gender.
- ☯ Discuss whether these perceptions are correct and how they are formed.

Religious overview

- ☯ Explore examples of the roles men and women play today in their faith communities.

Christian viewpoint

Christians believe that God created men and women to live together in harmony, to be a blessing to each other and to help each other. Although the culture in which Jesus grew up was male-dominated, he treated women with a respect beyond the norm for his day. There are many women of faith in the Bible, who are shown to be respected and accepted members of the faith community.

Do children agree with this viewpoint?

 Key Bible verses

God loves you and has chosen you as his own special people. So be gentle, kind, humble, meek, and patient. Put up with each other, and forgive anyone who does you wrong, just as Christ has forgiven you.

COLOSSIANS 3:12–13

Bible story link

In the Bible there is a story about a woman called Deborah, who was a respected civil administrator in Israel. She was also a prophetess and had the ability to discern God's will. Together with Barak, her army general, Deborah led a force of Israelite soldiers to defeat the opposing army of Sisera in northern Palestine. She told her people what God wanted them to do and led them to victory. (Story synopsis based on Judges 4:4–16.)

Teamwork

Early one Saturday morning, 13 people meet at Amersham station, which is at the end of Transport for London's Metropolitan line. They are going to spend their day travelling on the London underground network. Every station they go through will help to raise money for children who live on the streets of Guatemala in Central America.

Many children in Guatemala have been abandoned by their parents and have to beg or steal food and clothes to survive. The money the two teams raise will go towards building a new house for some of these children to live in.

'I've got 22 sponsors,' Sally says. 'Dad took my form to work and got lots of people to sponsor me.'

'I only managed five,' Kate sighs, 'but it'll be all right as long as we go to over 150 stations. Mum's promised me £100 if we do, but if we go to less, she's going to give me a fiver for the lot.'

'We should make it,' says Jane.

Jane is in charge of the girls' team. She helped with the

challenge last year, too. Her team had clocked up 185 stations by the end of the day.

'You might have won last year, but you won't win this year,' Lee sneers.

'Yeah!' Sam joins in. 'There's six of us in the boys' team and only five of you girls, so we're bound to win. Boys are better than girls, anyway.'

'Don't start that,' Mike says. He is in charge of the boys' team. 'We're here to raise money, not decide if boys are better than girls.'

'But boys are better, so there's nothing to discuss.'

At that moment the train appears, so everyone concentrates on getting on board. Each of the children has a map of the underground network and as the train passes through each station, they tick it off the list. Chalfont and Latimer, Chorleywood, Rickmansworth, Moor Park, Northwood and so on down the line to Wembley Park.

'Right, lads, we're getting off here,' Mike announces, and stands up.

'Are you going north on the Jubilee line to Stanmore?' Jane asks him.

Mike nods. 'Where are you heading for first?'

'Epping,' Jane says. 'We'll get one of the furthest ones done first.'

Mike grins. 'Have a nice day, anyway!' he says. 'See you later.'

The doors hiss as they open and the boys jostle their way off the train.

'Bet we'll beat you,' Lee whispers as he passes the girls.

Sally tries to kick him, only he jumps out of the way.

'I hate boys,' she says as the train pulls out of the station.

By eleven o'clock the girls are in Epping, with 34 stations ticked off. They have to wait 20 minutes until another train takes them back to Woodford and they can tick off the stations on the loop.

'I'm hungry,' Jo says, taking out her lunch box. She has enough sandwiches to keep them all going right through the day.

'Pity your mum didn't sponsor us for eating sandwiches,' Jane laughs.

Meanwhile, the boys have reached Morden, at the bottom of the Northern line. It is here that Mike really begins to embarrass them. He gets out a piece of cardboard. On it are the words, 'We're collecting money for street children in Guatemala. Tap my bald head and give generously. Thank you.'

Mike sits on the edge of his seat and holds the piece of cardboard so that everyone can see it. Joshua and Sam, who are sitting next to him, ask if they can get off the train and go it alone.

'No,' Mike says, 'we're here to raise money as a team, and this is one way of doing it.'

'Wish I'd gone with the others,' Joshua sighs.

'Not the girls! They're wimps!' Sam says, screwing his nose up. 'That reminds me, I heard a good joke last week. Why do women have small feet?'

'I don't know,' Lee joins in. 'Why do women have small feet?'

'So they can get closer to the kitchen sink!' Sam laughs.

'Eh?' Joshua says. He doesn't understand the joke.

'That's all women are good for,' Sam says to him. 'To be in the kitchen, wash up and stand by the sink. They're useless at doing anything else. Get it now?'

Joshua is not sure whether to laugh or not. His dad spends as much time in the kitchen as his mum does. He is about to say something about it when Mike chips in.

'That's enough,' he says. 'Those aren't real jokes. They're just you being nasty.'

Meanwhile, the girls are getting bored.

'Let's play *I spy*,' Jane says. But that's even more boring.

The boys are fed up, too, and they let everyone know about it. They end up making so much noise that all the other passengers get out and find another carriage to travel in. Then the boys get off the train and go to a burger bar for a snack. When they return to the underground they are armed with straws. They rip the clear plastic wrappers from the straws, tear them into little bits, chew them and then, when they are sure Mike isn't looking, load the soggy paper into one end of the straws before blowing down the other, taking aim at unsuspecting passengers.

Back with the girls there is real trouble, because the train they are travelling in breaks down only a few minutes after it has pulled out of Kew Gardens. They are completely stuck for over an hour. By the time they get off at the next station, find a loo and get back on another train, they have lost over an hour and a half.

'We'll never beat the boys now,' Lizzie groans. 'Why do they have to win? They'll say it's because we're girls and that we're sad and that they're better than us. But they're not better than us. Ever.'

By the end of the day, both teams are fed up. They meet at Baker Street station just after seven o'clock to travel back to Amersham together. The boys have been through 189 stations. The girls only have 149 ticked off.

'If we hadn't been in a train that broke down, we'd have had loads more stations,' Jane says sadly.

Mike is standing by Kate. She is very quiet.

'What's the matter?' he asks her.

'I didn't get 150 stations, so my mum will only give me five pounds,' she says.

'But you're only one away,' Mike says. 'Won't she imagine you've been to an extra one just to make the number up?'

'You don't know my mum,' Kate says. 'There's no way she'll change her mind.' Her voice trails off. She wants to cry because she is so tired and fed up, but she is determined not to in case she gets called a crybaby.

'Shall we count all the stations again and see if you've missed one?' Mike asks. He is really tired himself, but he can see that Kate is fighting back the tears and he wants to help her.

'All right,' Kate nods glumly and together they go through the girls' route very carefully. Suddenly Mike jumps up in the air. He has a habit of doing that when he gets excited about something.

'You haven't counted Amersham itself, have you?' he says with a huge grin on his face.

Kate looks at him. She looks at her piece of paper. Then she looks back at Mike again. He's right!

'That makes 150 and £100 from my mum,' she says.

'Brilliant!' Mike grins. 'That's going to make a huge difference to the amount of money your team raises. I expect you'll win now.'

'We've won really,' Sam and Lee say together, 'because we went to more stations than the girls did.'

'No, you haven't,' Jane says. She is tired of some of the things the boys have been saying. 'The real winners are the children in Guatemala. Because of what both teams have done. So there.'

Things children have said

'... boys are fun... stronger... tougher... Kind... good-looking... sporty... brilliant... bullies... clever... lazy... friendly...'

'... girls are silly... sissy... crybabies... gorgeous... stupid... perfume... clever and intelligent... hard-working...'

'... if you have a brother or a sister you think differently to someone who hasn't got any...'

'... you should all just be friends together...'

'... boys are stronger and better at football and know more about trains...'

'... boys are horrible because they make you embarrassed...'

'... sometimes boys can be funny. As long as you don't take them too far...'

'... my mum thinks boys are funny because she knows they're a load of rubbish...'

'... people are different. They're not better or worse. They're just different...'

'... girls are more precious...'

'... boys fight more to get their feelings out that way...'

'... girls are braver than boys because they have babies and have to look after them...'

'... they should cry the same amount because boys are still people and people cry because they're upset and crying helps you get better...'

'... girls are better because boys are lazy...'

'... boys are boys and girls are girls and that's it. They're the same at some things and different at others. But they're all good at something. None of them are actually better...'

Thinking time for children

If you think that either boys or girls are better, are you right? Why? Do you treat some people differently from others because they are a boy or a girl? Is this what you should be doing?

Thinking time activity

Make a list of things boys and girls do that are the same. Will they always be the same, or will the list change as you become older? Can you give a reason why?

Prayer

Dear God, help us to know if we say or do something that hurts someone else. Thank you that you love us all equally, no matter whether we are boys or girls. Amen

Making friends

Story summary

Urma joins a new Brownie pack where the welcome is best described as 'cold'. She and Mum discuss what Urma can do to make some new friends. The story tackles issues surrounding friendship, belonging and sharing.

RE concept: Belonging

 Exploring the concept

Children's understanding

- ❂ Talk about children's experiences of making friends and why we need friends.
- ❂ Discuss the importance of belonging to families and groups of people.
- ❂ Talk about how you know if you belong to something.

Religious overview

- ❂ Explore how belonging to a faith community offers friendship, shared values, identity and security.

Christian viewpoint

Christians believe that God wants people to support one another and work together for the common good. In this respect, the worldwide Church is seen as the family of God, to which all believers belong, each one a child in God's great family.

Do children agree with this viewpoint?

 Key Bible verse

The group of followers all felt the same way about everything. None of them claimed that their possessions were their own, and they shared everything they had with each other.

ACTS 4:32

 Bible story link

The early Christians belonged to each other. They supported one another and worked together, sharing what they owned, meeting to pray and learn about their new faith. Those on their own and children without parents were cared for by those who lived in families. (Story synopsis based on Acts 4:32–35.)

No one to play with

Urma was a Brownie. Where she used to live, she went to a Brownie pack that met on Thursdays, but Urma's family had just moved and her new pack met on a Wednesday evening. Urma's mum cooked tea extra early so she could be ready in time.

'I hope you enjoy it,' she said as they walked together to the hall where the Brownie pack met. Urma smiled. She loved Brownies. She loved the games and learning about different things and making new friends.

When she walked into the hall the meeting had already started.

'I must have got the time wrong,' Mum said. 'Urma, I'm so sorry.' Even then Urma didn't mind. The pack was playing Port and Starboard and she knew how to play, too. It was just a case of waiting for one of the adults to come and say 'hello' and let her join in. But no one bothered to come across and say 'hello' until the game had finished and everyone was laughing and sitting on the carpet in the corner. Then someone came across to them.

Mum left and Urma was taken over to Joanne, who was supposed to look after her. But Joanne kept forgetting to include her and started to chat with her own friends instead. Urma started to feel left out.

The Brownies were all working on their 'Friend to animals' interest badge. Urma did not know what to do. Everyone else did because they had been there last week. Brown Owl explained about making a book about animals for a young child. She asked

Joanne if she could help Urma with hers. Joanne smiled sweetly and said she would, but forgot all about Urma and carried on talking to her friends.

There were some books on the table. Urma looked through them and found a picture of a badger. She decided to draw that and found herself a piece of paper. No one had told her to bring a pencil case, so she picked up a felt-tipped pen that was lying on the table.

'Oi!' said a cross voice. 'That's mine. Go and get your own.'

'I only wanted to draw my badger,' Urma whispered, putting the felt-tipped pen back.

'I really want to go home,' she thought.

Urma flicked through the pages of the wild animal book. She was not very good at reading and the book had been written for grown-ups, not children, so she could not understand many of the words. She thought about her old Brownie pack. They always played games before they went home. Maybe they would here. Then she might have a chance to join in. But when they did play games, Urma did not know what to do and let her Six down.

'That new girl's useless,' someone said behind her back as they finished.

'Did you have a good time?' her mum asked a few minutes later. Urma shook her head and told her what had happened. Her mum sighed. Urma lifted her hand and let her fingers curl round Mum's as they walked along the road.

'You know what?' Mum said.

'What?' Urma asked.

'You could think of everyone at Brownies as being inside a circle. They all know each other because they've spent quite a bit of time together.'

Urma nodded.

'Now,' Mum carried on, 'imagine them inside the circle and you outside.'

'I just never want to go back there again,' Urma said.

'I know,' Mum sighed, 'but that's because you're still on the outside. You tried to get inside, but the circle didn't open up to let you in, did it?'

'No one talked to me or let me join in and they're all horrid,' Urma said.

They walked in silence for a while, past a row of shops and across Parkway Avenue.

'Tell you what,' said Mum. 'When we get home, I'll sew your new badge on so that everyone knows which Six you're in, and then next week we could ask one of the girls to come to tea beforehand so that you know one of them better than the others. I could phone up Brown Owl and ask her to suggest someone if you want. Then the circle will open up for you and you'll feel like you belong.'

Urma pulled a face. 'I don't like being on my own,' she said.

'Not many people do,' Mum replied. 'We're made so that we need to belong.'

Things children have said

'... I wouldn't go back to the Brownie pack if they were horrible to me...'

'... I'd want my mum to say something to the person who was running it and tell them how nasty everyone had been to me the week before...'

'... I'd go once more. You've got to give people a chance when you go somewhere new...'

'... I'm lonely in the playground...'

'... Louise in our road comes and plays with us and we try to be nice to her. But as soon as someone else comes that she likes better, she leaves us in the middle of our game, and then her mum gets cross with us because she thinks we won't play with her...'

Thinking time for children

Which groups do you belong to? What do you do to welcome new people into those groups? Think of three groups you belong to and work out which is the most important and why.

Thinking time activity

Draw a Venn diagram with each circle representing a group you belong to. Write the names of the people who belong inside the circles. Does anyone's name need to go in the overlapping sections?

Prayer

Dear God, you show us that we belong to you by loving us. Help us to do the same with people who join groups that we belong to, even if it's really hard to do. Amen

Emerging world issues

Story summary

The storyline jumps between Carlos, a street child in Guatemala, and Titch's family, who buy a barbecue set they don't need, then face a water leak that ruins their brand new carpets. The story focuses on issues of waste, inequality and fairness.

RE concept: Defending those who live in poverty

 Exploring the concept

Children's understanding

- Share experiences of when children have done something to help people less fortunate than themselves.
- Talk about why some people need support and care and who should help them.

Religious overview

- Explore how and why faith communities defend those who need support and care.

Christian viewpoint

Christians believe it is God's will that people who are disadvantaged in any way should be helped by those who are more fortunate. One of the major themes in the life and teaching of Jesus is the call for social justice and the need for people to help those less fortunate than themselves.

Do children agree with this viewpoint?

 Key Bible verses

Defend those who are helpless and have no hope. Be fair and give justice to the poor and homeless.

PROVERBS 31:8–9

 Bible story link

One day, a very rich man confronted Jesus. He wanted to know what he should do in order to have eternal life. Jesus said that the man should obey God's commandments, to which he replied that he had obeyed God's commandments since he was a child. Jesus told the man that the one thing he still needed to do was to sell everything he owned, give the money to the poor and follow Jesus. When the man heard this, he was very sad, because he was unable to give up his great wealth. Jesus made the comment that it is harder for a rich person to get into God's kingdom than for a camel to go through the eye of a needle. (Story synopsis based on Luke 18:18–25.)

The day the water fell

Guatemala is a beautiful country in Central America with high mountains, volcanoes, shimmering lakes and sandy beaches. It is also a very poor country. Many of the children do not go to school or have enough food to eat or water piped into their houses. Many of them do not even have houses.

Carlos lived in Guatemala. When he was six years old, his mother took him to the city and told him to wait by a bus stop. She disappeared into the crowd. He watched her go, but she never came back for him.

That evening he ended up at the city rubbish dump. Other children were there. They stared at him. Vultures circled over-head. Stinking rubbish was piled up in front of him. That night he slept under the open sky. The following morning he found some mouldy food. He ate it. Then he drank from a puddle. Carlos spent the day on the city streets. There was nowhere else to go.

'Please,' he begged, 'give me some money.'

Strangers spat at him; some of them kicked him and told him to get out of their way.

'I'm hungry,' he whispered.

'Go back home, then,' they said.

'I can't.'

Other children were begging as well. One of them grabbed a lady's handbag and started running, running as fast as he could. People joined in the chase. The child disappeared round a corner. So did the people. A police siren wailed. The children stopped begging and melted into the background. The police did not like beggars and street children. They moved them on and hit them. Sometimes they shot them.

Carlos ended up at the back of a restaurant. There were rubbish bags waiting to be taken to the dump. He opened one of them. No knife, no fork, no plate, no laughter, no love. Just Carlos pulling scraps of food from a rubbish bag.

One of the waiters from the restaurant had seen him. Carlos stood up and ran. There was nowhere he could think of to go. Not one place. No one wanted him. There were clouds in the sky. It would probably rain later. He must make sure he had somewhere to shelter.

Meanwhile, on the other side of the world, Titch's dad staggered into the kitchen with an enormous cardboard box.

'We had a man come to school with one of those,' Titch said. 'He told us about children who don't have homes to go to and end up living on the streets. They sleep in boxes like that.'

'Well, this one's got a barbecue in it,' Dad laughed. 'We don't need one, but it was on special offer so your mother had to buy it.'

'The man told us that...' Titch was going to carry on—only he stopped because Mum had let out an almighty scream.

'There's water dripping from the ceiling in the hall!' she yelled.

She was right. Titch could hear it, and he could see it cascading through the hole where the light-bulb cable was attached to the ceiling. It was quite exciting—just like their own personal waterfall.

'I think I'd better turn the water supply off,' Dad said calmly. He put the barbecue box down on the kitchen floor and headed for the cupboard under the sink. He found what he thought was the tap and gave it a firm twist. But the water carried on falling.

Dad stuck his head back in the cupboard and turned the tap again. The water still poured.

'Do something!' Mum wailed. 'My new carpet is getting ruined.'

'The only tap I know to turn the water off is the one under the sink,' Dad said. There was a slight panic in his voice and Mum had started to cry. She was not very good in an emergency.

'Don't cry,' Titch said. 'You'll make the carpet even wetter.'

Mum stared at him. Titch wished he had kept his mouth closed.

It was at that moment that the electric light bulb decided it did not like having water all over it and exploded. Four large fragments of glass sprayed themselves on to the carpet. At least no one was hurt. Mum screamed and Dad told her to pull herself together.

Titch stood where he was and watched. He was just wondering what was going to happen next when there was an enormous thud from the fuse box above the front door. That was 'goodbye' to the electricity, but not 'goodbye' to the water. It was still flowing, very cold and very wet. And then, because some water had got inside its control box in the hall, the burglar alarm started flashing.

'We've got one minute before the alarm starts ringing, and five before Mrs Hodge from next door comes round to complain,' Dad said. Unlike Mum, who was standing in the middle of the soggy carpet bawling her eyes out, he was still fairly calm. Titch was impressed.

'One, we stop the burglar alarm,' Dad said out loud. 'Two, we find the tap to turn off the water. Meanwhile, Titch, get two buckets out of the shed so that you and Mum can catch the water as it pours through the ceiling and empty them over the front garden.'

'If I were a street child, I wouldn't have to bother about Mum's new carpet because I wouldn't have one,' Titch thought. It was a funny thing to think as he opened the shed door. Titch's next thought was, 'That's one minute since the alarm triggered. Mrs Hodge will be round to complain about it, and it sounds like Dad can't stop it.'

'I'm going to phone for a plumber,' Mum shouted as she emptied her second bucket over a bush in the front garden. 'Titch, keep doing the buckets.'

'An emergency plumber should come straight away,' Dad muttered as he pressed the last button on the burglar alarm control panel and stood up. He had had to take the control panel to bits. The blue light stopped flashing. The siren stopped wailing. From the outside of the house, it looked as though Titch was in charge of watering the garden. No burglars, no panic and no Mrs Hodge.

In Guatemala, there was no panic either. The handbag had been given back to its owner and all the people had carried on with whatever they were doing. The police would send someone later in the day to remove the child's body. José had lived at the rubbish dump, and that's where he would be buried. A small mound of earth would be the only thing by which to remember him. No one bothered about these kids; they were just a nuisance.

'I'm all alone and I'm frightened,' Carlos whispered, but no one heard him. He was the same age as Titch, felt the warmth of the same sun, but their lives were so different.

❖

Back in England, things were looking up. The burglar alarm was off, Mrs Hodge had still not appeared (because she was out shopping for a new set of table and chairs), Titch was catching most of the water in the buckets and Mum had at last found an emergency plumber who did not have his answer machine on.

'An hour is too long,' she shouted down the phone. 'There's water all over the place, the light bulb has exploded and the burglar alarm has gone off. I don't care how much you charge as long as you get here before my house is completely ruined.'

The plumber said he would get there as soon as he could. Mum did not believe him, so she kept trying until she found another plumber who answered the telephone. He, too, said he would come.

'The plumbers keep telling me the tap is in the cupboard under the sink,' she yelled.

'But it's not there,' Dad shouted down from the loft. 'That was the first place I tried.'

Mum punched some more numbers into the phone. Nine. Nine. Nine.

'The tap is always under the sink,' the police told her, 'and no, we do not deal with water leaks. Have you thought of contacting the water board?'

'No!' she snapped back.

'I'm going to have one last look under the sink,' Dad said, coming down the stairs. He had banged his head on the loft hatch and was not happy. 'Come and help me, Titch.'

Titch handed Mum the bucket he was holding.

'I'm going to empty the cupboard,' Dad said, and began passing boxes and tins to Titch. The very last thing he took out was a huge box of washing powder. Underneath where it had stood was a hole, neatly cut in the base of the cupboard. Inside the hole was... a little tap. Dad twiddled his fingers and... Silence. Total silence. For a brief second, everyone closed their eyes and enjoyed it until Dad shouted, 'Yahoo!'

'So what about the tap you turned in the first place?' Mum asked.

Dad put his hand to his mouth. 'I am daft!' he said. 'That's the tap that feeds the washing machine.'

Mum said something very rude.

'At least the water's off,' Dad snapped back.

'But my carpet's ruined,' Mum cried.

'It'll dry,' Dad said. 'Can you cancel one of those plumbers? We need one to sort out the leak, not two.'

Mum opened her mouth. Then she closed it. Then she opened it again. Titch thought it was a very good impression of a goldfish. Maybe the water was getting to her.

'I can't remember who I phoned,' she whispered. 'I just went through the Yellow Pages and called every plumber I came to.'

'You did what? You don't know who's coming?'

'No.'

'And how much do they charge just to turn up at our house?'

Mum told him.

It was Dad's turn to say something rude.

'At least Mrs Hodge didn't come round,' Titch said.

'I think we all need a hot drink,' Dad said. But the kettle wouldn't boil, because the electric wiring was still soaking wet.

'I think we're going to need an electrician, too,' Dad wailed.

Just then there was a knock at the door.

'Is that Mrs Hodge, or is it the plumber?' Mum wondered.

'Plumber, I hope,' Titch said.

It was. Ten minutes later, there was another knock at the

door. The second plumber was told he was not needed. The second plumber was not a happy plumber.

'It's come on to rain,' Mum said as she shut the front door. 'No need to water the plants tonight.'

❖

It was also raining in Guatemala. Carlos watched the little circles dancing in the puddle. At least he'd have something to drink in the morning.

Things children have said

'... this story is sad. I wish I could help...'

'... I don't need all my toys, clothes, shoes, electrical stuff, calendars, clothes that are too small, old light bulbs, food like chocolate biscuits...'

'... we have too many towels at home...'

'... our dog and my brother's pet rat. I hate it...'

'... television, radio, hi-fi, games for my computer. We don't actually need them, but they are nice to have...'

'... we have money, education, friends and SATs practice tests, only they're stupid...'

'... clean clothes, CDs, a dad or mum, food, drink, PlayStation, clean water, toothbrush...'

'... someone who cares for me and protects me, someone to tell me what to do, what is right and wrong...'

'... everyone should respect everyone else...'

'... because we should be kind to each other...'

'... no one bothers about other people who don't have any money, though we ought to because poor people are still humans like we are...'

'... the poor don't wash properly because they can't get water. Then people don't go near them because they smell. But that's not fair and it's not right either...'

Thinking time for children

Think of all the things that street children like Carlos do not have. Can you think of any ways you can help children who do not have as many things as you? What could our country do to help?

Thinking time activity

Draw pictures of all the things you have that someone like Carlos does not have. Put them in order of importance.

Prayer

Dear God, we have so many things that we take for granted. Help us to appreciate them. Help us to be generous and to thank you for all we have. Amen

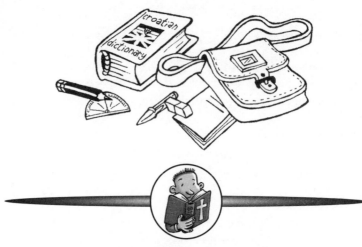

Cultural differences

Story summary

Robbie's father has taken up a lecturing post at Zagreb university, so the family moves from America to live in Croatia. Robbie does not find the move easy. The story explores how cultural differences can be a positive experience if all parties make allowances and accept each other.

RE concept: Accepting other people

 Exploring the concept

Children's understanding
❂ Talk about what it must be like to arrive in a completely new environment where everything seems to be different.

Religious overview
❂ Explore how people from different cultures and religions can show respect for and acceptance of each other's ways of life.

Christian viewpoint
Christians believe that God created the world and every living thing. God's love reaches to every corner of the world and he is always with them even when they are far from home.

Do children agree with this viewpoint?

 Key Bible verse

You notice everything I do and everywhere I go.
PSALM 139:3

 Bible story link

In the Bible, Abram (later called Abraham) is told by God to leave his country, his family and his relatives and go to the land that God will show him. Life was not always easy for Abram, but as he travelled he learned many things about God. (Story synopsis based on Genesis 12:1–9.)

It's so different

Croatia is a very special place. At least, that was what Robbie's mother told him. A lady in a huge coat smiled at them as they came down the steps from the aeroplane.

'Dobro dan,' she greeted everyone. 'Welcome to Zagreb.'

The air was cold. Robbie could see his breath in it.

'I think "dobro dan" means "hello",' his mother whispered —not that Robbie was listening. He had spotted the cream-and-green military helicopters in a field nearby, their rotor blades dangling loosely from a central metal column. There was something threatening and nasty about them.

He wanted to be back in America, back with his friends, his house with its kidney-shaped swimming pool and streets with restaurants and fast cars zigzagging up the highway. Only he was here, aged nine, on what he had been told was an exciting adventure—which really meant he had to learn another language, meet lots of new people, leave all his friends behind and find out what life was like in a different part of the world.

Dad would still be working at a university where most people spoke English and Mum would still be writing news-paper articles, just as she did back home. It was all right for them. He was the one going to a new school. What if the other children didn't like him because he was American? He'd seen a programme on television once about people from different countries not being liked just because of where they came from. It didn't matter what the person was like—if they came from the wrong country everyone was horrible to them. That might happen to him.

Robbie was so tired. All he wanted was his bed, his nice comfy bed, back in America. But there was Dad, waiting for them, grinning and smiling and coming towards them with his arms out for a hug. He had been in Zagreb, the capital of Croatia, for a month already.

'You'll love the apartment,' Dad told them as he swung their suitcases into the back of his car. 'And, Robbie, the school you're going to is just fine. I went there last week and spoke to the principal. You'll have English lessons, which you'll find dead easy, and they're going to give you extra lessons to help you learn to speak Croatian.'

Extra lessons. Who wanted those? Robbie certainly didn't!

They were driving along a fast road now. Robbie looked at the adverts along the side of it. The letters had squiggles sticking up and hanging down from them. He was going to have to learn what they meant.

'I want to go back home,' he whispered to himself. 'Please, let me go back.'

It only took 15 minutes to reach the block of apartments where they would be living. Old cars littered the street, but there was a park at the far end. Maybe he could play baseball there—or maybe not.

The tiny lift up to their apartment was plastered in graffiti and smelt dirty. At the second floor, the lift doors opened and Robbie just had time to see a concrete landing before the lights went out.

'Stay here and I'll put the lights back on,' Dad said and disappeared into the semi-darkness. 'We have one minute before they go off again,' he said ten seconds later.

Paint was peeling off the iron railings by the stairs, and it felt cold. 'That's our door,' Dad pointed out, 'at the far end of the landing. Be quick, or the lights will go out again.' He helped them with their cases and then took out the key.

To Robbie's surprise, the apartment was all right. It was smaller than their house in America, but very cosy. Robbie had a computer in his bedroom and he could see the park from his window. Some children were playing football.

Dad had a meal ready for them, but the food tasted odd and neither Robbie nor Mum was hungry. They had been travelling for 17 hours and all they really wanted to do was go to bed and sleep.

That is exactly what they did, but the following morning Robbie and Mum both overslept. Their bodies were still on American time. Robbie shut his eyes and wished he were back home again.

That day, he and Mum got used to their new home and fought off the deep feelings of wanting to fall asleep. In the afternoon they visited the market in the middle of Zagreb. It was full of vegetables and fruit, all laid out on tables. Mum bought some figs and then got confused with the different money she now had to use. Then they went to the cathedral behind the market. It had lots of gold paintings and stained-glass windows and pictures, and was a bit like the one back home. There was something nice about that.

On Monday, Dad took Robbie to his new school. There were 25 other children in his class. The teacher smiled at him. She spoke a little English and asked Miro to look after him.

'Dobro dan,' Miro said and smiled in a friendly sort of way. That was what the lady at the airport had said to them.

'Dow–bro dan,' Robbie tried back. But everyone was laughing at him. Was it because he had tried to speak their language and got it wrong?

'Dobro,' Miro repeated slowly. 'D–o–bro.'

He made the 'o' sound short as in 'ox'.

'Dobro,' Robbie said. Miro put his thumb up and smiled again.

Once Robbie was settled in, the teacher carried on with the lesson—in Croatian. Robbie looked at the pictures in the books they were using. There were maps, so he decided it was a geography lesson. When everyone started writing, the teacher came to his table and tried to explain it to him, only her English wasn't that good.

By the end of his first day at school, Robbie had learned how to say three very important words: 'please' (*molim*), 'thank you' (*hvala*) and 'toilet' (*toaleta*). He also liked the fact that his new school had a break at ten o'clock for a snack (he had pizza and chips) and finished lessons at lunchtime, with clubs in the afternoon. He played football with Miro and some of the other boys and was as good as, if not better than, most of them.

'Well,' Mum said, when he arrived back at the apartment, 'how was it?'

Robbie screwed his nose up. It had been 'all right' but not brilliant. It could have been worse, and tomorrow he would learn some more new words. But for now, he was going to bed—to sleep.

Things children have said

'... Mum needs to let him bring his new friends back to where they live...'

'... he should only be spoken to in Croatian, then he would have to learn...'

'... the language will be the hardest because you can't see it...'

'... every country has its own traditions and he won't know any of those and will feel left out...'

'... he might insult someone and not realize it...'

'... they might not like him because he's American...'

'... he won't be able to make them laugh *because* they won't understand him, and if they don't laugh they won't relax with him...'

'... he should have someone sit next to him and translate what the teacher says into his own language until he understands. Then he'd learn really quickly...'

'... he needs to know the language and he might come *back* to the country when he is older...'

Thinking time for children

Do you know anyone who has come from another country? How did they get on when they first arrived? What would help someone the most? How would you feel if you were Robbie and everything seemed to be different from what you were used to?

Thinking time activity

Make a list of the ten things you would find hard if you went to live in another country. Put them in order, with the hardest things at the top of the list.

Prayer

Dear God, it's hard when we go to new places, especially if we can't understand what is happening. There are many people facing that today. Help those they are with to be kind and patient. Amen

Media headlines

Story summary

Azad's paper round includes going to the house of the famous football player, Kevin Swingot. One morning, Azad realizes there has been a robbery and alerts the police. The news hits the headlines of the local press—only not everything that is reported is correct. The story encourages children to think about truth and whether what they hear in the media (and from other people) is correct.

RE concept: Truth

 Exploring the concept

Children's understanding

❂ Compare recent headlines and stories in newspapers and magazines and discuss in what ways they are different or the same.

❂ Talk about what truth is.

❂ Discuss whether it is important always to tell the truth and how that impacts on other people and relationships.

Religious overview

❂ Explore how faith communities deal with dishonesty, and how truth and trust are linked in religious belief.

Christian viewpoint

Christians believe that God wants people to be honest with each other and tell the truth, and that God will bless those who are honest and fair in everything they do.

Do children agree with this viewpoint?

 Key Bible verse

Do not tell lies about others.

EXODUS 20:16

 Bible story link

Jesus told a story about a farmer who sowed seed in his field. The seed was likened to truth about God being sown into people's lives. Some of the farmer's seed fell on to the path and birds ate it. Some fell among stones, where there was little soil. The plants grew, but were quickly scorched by the sun. Other seed fell where there were thorn bushes and the thorns choked the plants. But some of the seed fell on good soil and produced corn. This seed represents the people who accept the truth of God's word with good and honest hearts. (Story synopsis based on Mark 4:1–9.)

Ali's forty thieves

Azad loved doing his newspaper round. He loved it for two reasons. One, he got paid. Two, Kevin Swingot's house was on his round. That was something special, because Kevin Swingot played football—and we're not talking first or second division here, we're talking Premiership.

Every morning, Azad would walk up the long sweeping drive towards Kevin's house, hoping to see the footballer going for an early morning jog with his three Labradors and his personal trainer, or a glimpse of the beautiful Lucy Swingot, Kevin's wife, who was a model. Only he never did, because Kevin Swingot had another house that was even bigger and better, and he actually lived in that house. The newspapers Azad delivered were for Mr Jones the caretaker, who looked after the house when Kevin wasn't living there.

It was a Friday when it happened, just after seven o'clock as Azad walked up the drive. He heard what sounded like glass being broken, coming from the back of the house. Now Azad's dad was a policeman and always said that if Azad came across anything unusual that might be dangerous, he was not to get involved or try to be a hero. His dad had also given him a mobile phone, but Azad had forgotten to charge it up last night so it was lying on the table in his bedroom, plugged into the mains. Typical, the one day when he might need it!

So Azad stopped where he was and coughed very loudly, just to let whoever it was know that someone else was there. Then he hurtled as fast as he could back down the drive and waved frantically at the first car that came along. The driver pulled over.

'What's up?' asked a young man in a smart suit, leaning over the passenger seat.

'That's Kevin Swingot's house,' Azad panted.

'What? *The* Kevin Swingot?'

Azad nodded. 'Someone's just broken a window... at the back of the house... my dad says I should call the police.'

'Where is your dad, then?'

'At home.'

'Is he famous, too?'

'No, he's a policeman.'

'We'd better do it, then. Are you sure it was glass you heard?'

'Well, I think so... It was round the back of the house and I was at the front, going to deliver the newspaper.'

The young man pulled out his mobile phone and called 999. Three minutes and 22 seconds later, a police car zoomed round the corner with all its lights flashing and sirens blaring. Azad stood by the gates as the car swept up the drive. He then watched as two policemen got out and disappeared round the back of the house. Azad decided to wander back up the drive—after all, he still had a newspaper to deliver.

'You're a smart one,' the police said to Azad when they reappeared a few minutes later. 'It looks like they broke the glass and then ran off. They left a trowel behind. Hopefully, there'll be some fingerprints on that. Well done, young man.'

Azad smiled. He told the police exactly what he had heard and seen, which wasn't much but was better than nothing.

'And is Kevin Swingot inside the house?' Azad asked, hopefully, as they finished.

The policeman shook his head. 'We woke the caretaker. He was asleep on the other side of the house when it happened and didn't hear anything.' The policeman wrote down Azad's name and address, thanked him again and said he could carry on with his paper round.

About ten minutes later, a woman dressed in jeans and a polo-neck jumper walked towards him. She had a notebook in her hand and a camera bag slung over her shoulder.

'Moira Johnston, reporter,' she introduced herself and tried to shake Azad's hand. 'I hear there's been a break-in at the Swingots' house. Is that right? Are you the paper boy who found the thieves?'

Azad stopped walking and nodded.

'You called 999 at five past seven and it's five to eight now,' she carried on. 'Were the police slow in answering your call?'

'No,' he said, glancing at his watch to check the time. He was running late and would get into trouble if he were late for school. So he answered 'yes', 'no' or 'I can't remember' to all the questions Moira Johnston asked him, and after a couple of minutes she left him alone.

Azad finished his paper round as quickly as he could and was only 15 minutes late when he got home. He told his mum what had happened.

'Well done,' she said when he finished. 'I'm proud of you. Dad will be, too. You're so sensible.'

Mum and Dad weren't the only ones who were proud. The local newspaper was as well. *Ali's forty thieves* the headline read the following evening.

Ten-year-old Azad Ali stopped thieves in their tracks at footballer Kevin Swingot's house yesterday. The brave newspaper boy disturbed their night's thieving when he heard glass being shattered. He raced to the road and flagged down a passing car, driven by George Holmes, 22, of

Stockton Lane. Mr Holmes, manager of Passports Suitcase Superstore, said it could have been very dangerous but Azad was not worried about his own safety and simply wanted the thieves caught and punished. Azad borrowed Mr Holmes' mobile phone to call the police station and then waited for over 20 minutes for them to arrive. In spite of police promises to arrive at crime scenes as quickly as possible, this was a long delay.

After giving a description of the thieves to the police, Azad continued his newspaper round before going to school. Azad knew what to do because his father, Constable Ali, 54, works for the local police force and had told his son exactly what to do. Mr Swingot was delighted that the thieves were thwarted and is going to offer brave Azad a reward.

'You're 44,' Mum howled with laughter, 'not 54.'

'Huh!' Dad said. 'And has Kevin Swingot offered you a reward? Because if he has, you haven't told us about it.'

'I haven't heard a thing,' Azad said. But maybe Kevin Swingot would feel he had to reward him now.

'How did that reporter know you were a policeman, Dad? I never told her,' he said.

His father looked at him. 'Did you tell George Holmes, 22, of Stockton Lane, manager of Passports Suitcase Superstore, that I was one?'

Azad frowned. 'Yes, I did,' he said slowly.

Dad sighed. 'The press find out all sorts of things about all sorts of people. Sometimes it's a good thing and stops people doing things they shouldn't do. Sometimes it's a bad thing.'

'Well, they've got a lot of the facts wrong in this story,' Mum laughed.

Thinking time for children

How important is it always to tell the truth? Why do the media sometimes give their audience information that is later shown to be incorrect? Why do people contact newspapers with stories about other people? Would you tell a reporter about your best friend if your best friend had done something the press might be interested in? Why or why not?

Thinking time activity

Write your own accurate article about what Azad actually did. Then write one that doesn't quite tell the truth.

Prayer

Dear God, help me always to tell the truth and never be disloyal to people who trust me. Amen

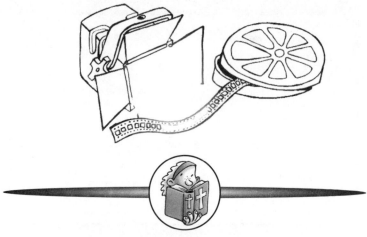

Challenging stereotypes

Story summary

The characters in the first-aid film being shot in Super Sofa Warehouse are all stereotypes, ranging from a tramp to a smartly dressed woman who bosses everyone around. The story addresses how and why people make value judgments about others.

RE concept: Judgment

 Exploring the concept

Children's understanding

- Talk about what it means to make a judgment about something or someone.

Religious overview

- Explore how faith communities view God as the ultimate judge.

Christian viewpoint

Christians believe it is God's will for people to treat others as they themselves would want to be treated and not to make value judgments based on appearances. Christians believe that one day everyone will have to stand before God and give an account of their behaviour—every hidden action and secret thought—because these are evidence of what a person is really like.

Do children agree with this viewpoint?

 Key Bible verses

Jesus said, 'Don't condemn others, and God won't condemn you. God will be as hard on you as you are on others! He will treat you exactly as you treat them.'

MATTHEW 7:1–2

 Bible story link

In the Bible there is a story about a young shepherd boy named David. At that time, the Israelite army was under attack from the Philistines. The Philistine army had a hero named Goliath, who was from the town of Gath. Goliath was a great giant of a man and a fearless soldier. David was incensed that Goliath was making fun of the Israelite army and volunteered to take him on. Goliath was expecting a man to fight him and laughed when he saw the young shepherd boy standing up to him, armed with nothing but a simple home-made catapult. But Goliath's value judgment about David proved to be very wrong and it cost him his life. (Story synopsis based on 1 Samuel 17:1–50.)

A time to change your mind

The old tramp's head hit the floor as he tripped and fell. Sharon the shop assistant raced forward.

'Ohh!' she cried, pushing her hair behind her ears so she could see the man better.

'He's fainted, hasn't he?' one of the other shoppers said, pushing forward to have a better look.

'We'd better do something, hadn't we?' Sharon said slowly. Then she pulled a face. She was going to have to touch him. At that point, a lady carrying a large blue handbag bustled forward and joined the others kneeling beside the man.

'Oh!' she said in a posh voice. 'All he needs is a good slap across the cheeks. Wake up, old man! You're not on the streets now! You're in a shop that sells sofas. Wake up!'

And with that, she slapped him twice across the cheek. Other shoppers, who had gathered round to have a look, glanced at each other, then back at the lady.

'Wake up! You've just had too much to drink, that's all. Can someone fetch a glass of water? That's all he needs, then he can be on his way and we can get on with our shopping.'

'I'll go,' Sharon whispered. She wasn't very good with people who were ill, and there was something about that large blue handbag and the way its owner spoke that made her a bit nervous. 'Shall I call an ambulance?' she mumbled. 'He could be really ill.'

'He is just a homeless tramp. Why are you suggesting we call an ambulance for him? He doesn't deserve one!' The woman's voice was shrill as she slapped the man across the cheek again.

There was a gasp from the other shoppers, but none of them offered to help. They just stood watching until Sharon tottered back on her high heels, carrying a glass of water. The old man's head lolled from side to side as the woman with the blue handbag lifted his shoulders and tried to make him sit up before trying to pour water into his mouth. The tramp coughed and spluttered, then rolled back on to the floor again.

'Shouldn't you stick his legs in the air?' someone said. 'You could drag him over there and stick them up on one of the sofas.'

There was a murmur of agreement from those watching and several hands began dragging him towards an orange leather sofa.

'I a nurse... You wrong... Check he breathe... Look at chest... Go up and down? Check pulse, but leave him on floor... No water.'

The young woman's gently spoken words were ignored as the woman with the blue handbag glanced over her shoulder and scowled.

'We know what we're doing, thank you very much. And I wouldn't listen to you anyway,' she added. 'You should go back to wherever you came from.'

The young woman didn't say anything further but stood watching the tramp, who now had his feet up on the sofa. The woman with the blue handbag was trying to pour some more water down his throat. Someone else stepped forward, a man in a suit.

'I went on a first-aid course once,' he said, 'and they told us to put someone who has fainted in the recovery position and open the airways so they can breathe properly. Why don't you listen to this young woman? She is a nurse.'

Everyone froze and looked at the young woman as she moved to the front again so that the camera could focus on her face.

'If someone collapse, no water…' She shook her head from side to side. 'No sit up unless it is heart attack. You do ABC. Airways. Are they clear? Breathing. Can you hear? Circulation. Find pulse.'

'And cut! Well done, everyone. That part of the film is fine now. After lunch, we'll show what to do when someone has a heart attack.'

The woman with the blue handbag began helping the old man off the floor, laughing as she did so.

'Are you all right, Sid?' She still had a posh voice, but now it was friendly and warm, not cruel and bossy as it had been a minute ago. 'I didn't slap you too hard, did I?'

'No,' the tramp grinned back. 'Come on, let's go and see what they've got for lunch today. You coming, Emma?'

The shop assistant kicked her high heels off and left them on one of the sofas in the studio.

'Beat you down there!' she cried, and broke into a run.

Things children have said

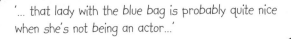

'... that lady with the *blue bag* is probably quite nice when she's not being an actor...'

'... it's very important to think *before* you speak...'

'... the film they're making is really offensive to all sorts of people...'

'... I felt sorry for the nurse. That *blue handbag* lady was horrible to her...'

'... don't judge a *book* by its cover...'

'... you need to know all the facts *before* you judge someone...'

'... I'd want to tell the lady with the *blue handbag* she was pompous and *bossy* and should listen to other people...'

'... she was mean, *selfish* and opinionated. I don't like her...'

'... tell her to get a life...'

'... stop being so moody and take people as they are. Everyone's a person and equal to everyone else...'

'... homeless people had homes once. Only sometimes they weren't very nice homes. That's why they left them. It's not always their fault...'

Thinking time for children

What judgments do you make about what other people look like... speak like... dress like...? Do you always make sure you know all the true facts before you make a judgment about someone or something? How do you think people see you? Do you ever wish the way they see you was different? What does the word 'stereotype' mean?

Thinking time activity

Act out the sort of situations Jesus was referring to in Matthew 7:1–2. In the Good News Bible these verses read, 'Do not judge others, so that God will not judge you, for God will judge you in the same way as you judge others, and he will apply to you the same rules you apply to others.'

Prayer

Dear God, it's easy to believe what people tell us, even if it's not the truth. Help us to find out the truth before we make a judgment. Amen

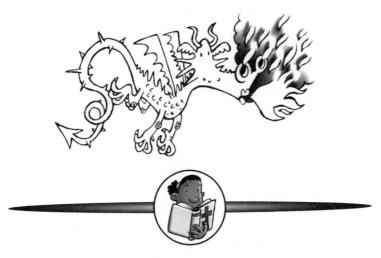

Fairness

Story summary

Hamlet, the beautiful princess's pet dragon, will have to remain in the castle when the royal family move, because their new castle has its own dragon—a fiery little thing whose fire won't go out. The story confronts issues of fairness and seeking solutions to put wrong things right.

RE concept: Justice

 ## Exploring the concept

Children's understanding

○ Explore what the children understand by the word 'justice'.

○ Talk about experiences children have had of fair and rough justice.

○ Talk about rules that children think are not fair and explore why this is.

Religious overview

○ Explore how faith communities deal with issues of justice.

Christian viewpoint

Christians believe that God has given each person a conscience so that they can tell the difference between right and wrong. It is a person's conscience that helps them to discern whether something is fair. Christians believe that God is always fair in the way he treats people.

Do children agree with this viewpoint?

 ## Key Bible verse

'Please make me wise and teach me the difference between right and wrong.'

1 KINGS 3:9a

 ## Bible story link

King Solomon was known to be very wise. One day he had a difficult case to judge. Two women had both had babies, but one of the babies had died. Each claimed that the surviving child was hers. They asked King Solomon to decide which of them was the true mother. The king sent for a sword and ordered the living baby to be cut in half. The real mother begged for the child not to be killed, but instead be given to the other woman. So King Solomon ordered the child to be left unharmed and given to the mother who had been prepared to let the baby go in order for it to live. (Story synopsis based on 1 Kings 3:16–28.)

The dragon with too much fire

There was once a beautiful princess who lived in a castle where half the walls had fallen down, the moat flooded whenever it rained, and the dragon, who went by the name of Hamlet, had stopped breathing fire and become the princess's pet.

Everything was wonderful until one day the princess's father said, between mouthfuls of spaghetti bolognaise and cheese, 'This castle is falling down. It is too old, too draughty and too big. Your mother and I have decided we are going to move.'

The beautiful princess gasped. 'Where are we moving to?' she asked in a dramatic voice. Her voice was trembling because a terrible thought was crawling across her brain. You see, every castle had its own dragon and, if they moved, Hamlet would have to stay in the old castle, even though it was falling down. That would be unbearable.

'Now don't go getting upset, my little princess,' the queen soothed. 'We've found a nice castle that has just been built. You'll have a bigger bedroom and it's only on the other side of the mountain, so you'll still be able to see your friends. We know you'll like it when you see it.'

The beautiful princess could stand it no longer. 'Uhh! Parents! You just don't understand,' she sobbed and fled from the table. She ran across the courtyard to the tower, threw open the door and raced up the spiral staircase to her bedroom. Hamlet was there, gazing out of the window at the buttercups swaying in the gentle breeze.

'Nice day today,' he breathed. 'Fancy a ride later on?'

'Oh Hamlet,' the beautiful princess gasped, 'the royal mummy and daddy have said they want to move. If we do, you have to stay here in this castle—and there is no way I am going to leave you behind, for you are my dearest dragon and my most perfect pet. I will refuse to move, even if they send for the royal guards!'

Hamlet lowered his neck and stared at her through sad eyes.

'Where do they want to move to?' he asked slowly.

'The new castle on the other side of the mountain.'

'Nice castle,' he breathed. 'I flew over it the other day. There's an indoor swimming pool with bright orange slides, six bedrooms with fitted wardrobes and en suite bathrooms, a large moat with ducks, a private cinema and central heating. You'll like it.'

'But I won't if you're not there, Hamlet.'

'Who says I won't be there?'

'Because this is your castle! This is the only castle you can ever live in. You will die if you leave. It's not fair and no one seems bothered about it.'

Hamlet frowned. He agreed. It didn't seem fair that dragons had to stay in just one castle, but those were the rules. But he was an upbeat sort of dragon, so he sighed and did his best to cheer up the beautiful princess.

'Come on,' he said, 'hop on my back. Let's go and have a look at the new castle. You never know what might happen.'

It was, indeed, a fantastic castle. The walls weren't falling down and the roof tiles were all different colours. Better still, the windows were double-glazed so the wind wouldn't come howling into all the rooms.

'So where's this castle's dragon?' Hamlet mused as they

circled above it. 'There must be one for it to be a proper castle. I'll give that dragon a shout and tell him he's got visitors. Cover your ears up... I'm about to shout!'

Even Hamlet, with all his hundreds and hundreds of years of experience, did not expect what happened next. For out of the well in the middle of the courtyard a ball of fire suddenly shot into the air. The ball of fire was about five metres long and it was spinning and twisting and making a terrible racket. Through the flames could be seen a very little dragon with a bluey-grey body, pointed spikes and horns.

'Wow!' the beautiful princess gasped. She grabbed hold of Hamlet's back to steady herself as Hamlet opened his wings wide to shield her from the fiery blast.

'Sure is some dragon,' he gulped. 'Oi! You! Come and say "hello" and put your fire away. I don't want my wings turned into toast.'

The new castle's little dragon hovered near them. 'Sorry,' she squeaked, 'but my fire won't go out.'

The beautiful princess and Hamlet stared at her.

'What's the matter with your voice?' Hamlet asked, trying not to laugh. Dragons didn't squeak; they roared.

'When the dragon makers made me,' she said, 'they ran out of voices. This was the only one they had left, so it was this or nothing. They gave me extra fire instead to make up for it, but it just makes things worse. I have to live in the well, otherwise I burn myself.'

'That's not fair!' cried the beautiful princess. She felt very sorry for this poor little dragon, and Hamlet was so sad that he let out an almighty roar.

'I'll never be able to do that,' the little dragon squeaked in her high-pitched voice, rather pathetically. 'My fire is here to stay for ever.'

'She's like a flying bonfire,' Hamlet mused. 'She'd be great for having barbecues.'

'We are going to have to do something to help you,' the beautiful princess said kindly.

'Oh!' squeaked the little dragon. 'I'm sorry, but I'm going to have to go back to the well. My claws are beginning to melt.' And with that, she plummeted back down and disappeared into the well she had shot out of two minutes earlier.

'Poor little thing!' the beautiful princess sighed. 'We have got to help her.'

That night, the beautiful princess tossed and turned in her bed, unable to sleep. Her world was suddenly filled with the injustice of it all. First of all, she was being forced to move and leave her beloved Hamlet behind. Now here was this poor little dragon who had to live in a well. Things were not improved by Hamlet's snoring on the other side of her room, which was also keeping her awake.

Just then, an owl hooted outside her bedroom window. It was at that moment that a thought blew into her brain. It made her jump out of bed and shake Hamlet's ears.

'Hamlet, wake up!'

'Eeehg!'

'Wake up! Tell me something. Years ago, you used to breathe fire, didn't you?'

'Eeehg!'

'Then you stopped breathing fire. Tell me. Why did you stop?'

'It was so long ago, I can hardly remember. Let me think... oh yes, I remember...'

Hamlet went pink all over and looked at the floor. 'I... I... fell in love,' he whispered.

'You fell in love! Who with?'

'That would be telling.'

'It would—and you're going to tell me now!'

Hamlet stretched his neck out and rested it across the floor.

'She was the most gorgeous dragon I've ever seen,' he said

sadly. 'Very beautiful, with an ice-cold tail. But she fell in love with George, the dragon from a castle 500 miles away. She married him instead. It was all such a long time ago and I'd rather not talk about it.'

'You've never told me that before,' the beautiful princess said, and she put her arms round Hamlet's shoulders and hugged him.

'You never asked.'

'And your fire went out when you fell in love?'

Hamlet nodded. 'It's called self-preservation. You can't kiss someone if you're breathing fire over them, can you?'

The princess thought about that one. Hamlet was right.

'But what happened when they got married? She couldn't leave her castle and neither could George.'

'Oh no. There's an ancient law that says if two dragons get married, one of them is allowed to leave their castle.'

'That's simple, then,' the beautiful princess smiled. 'After all, this is a fairy tale and who knows what might happen!'

Things children have said

'... I know what being fair is, but I'm not sure about what justice means...'

'... it's horrible when something isn't fair...'

'... no one should get a privilege when they've done nothing to deserve it...'

'... something's got to be changed if it's wrong and unfair...'

'... people who believe in God learn what is right from God...'

Thinking time for children

What do you think the word 'fair' means? How do you make sure what you do is fair when you're watching television with someone else? When you're playing in the playground? When you want to talk to your teacher but someone else is ahead of you? When a friend falls over in the middle of a game?

Thinking time activity

Write your own ending to the story, giving it:

a) An ending that is fair (or unfair) to both of the dragons.
b) An ending where the king does something that is wrong (or right).
c) An ending where the beautiful princess, Hamlet or the little dragon do something they like (or dislike) doing.

Work out how to share a round cake, a packet of chips and a plate of baked beans between seven friends and yourself.

Act out and hotseat the characters in the story of King Solomon and the two women, up to the point where the king has to decide what to do with the baby. Decide what should happen next. Is what actually happened next the best solution?

Prayer

Dear God, it's hard always to be fair. Help me to have the courage to make sure everyone is treated the same. Help me to know the difference between right and wrong. Give me the courage to do the right thing. Amen

Personal life

Understanding more about God

Story summary

This simple story is about a woman who walks her dog in the local park. During the walk, she marvels at the beauty of creation and wonders whether God exists. The story raises questions about spirituality and belief in God.

RE concept: The existence of God

 Exploring the concept

Children's understanding

- ◎ Talk about reasons why people do or don't believe in God.
- ◎ Discuss the basic belief systems of the major faiths.
- ◎ Write letters to people who will be able to tell the children about their faith, enclosing a stamped addressed envelope for answers.

Religious overview

- ◎ Explore how people of different faiths understand and explain the existence of God.

Christian viewpoint

Christians believe that God is everywhere, that he loves everything and everyone he has created, and that he created the world for everyone's enjoyment. Although they cannot fully understand God, Christians believe that they can see God in the world he has created and know his presence in their hearts and lives. One day people will see God face to face.

Do children agree with this viewpoint?

 Key Bible verse

Now all we can see of God is like a cloudy picture in a mirror. Later we will see him face to face. We don't know everything, but then we will, just as God completely understands us.

1 CORINTHIANS 13:12

Bible story link

In the Bible there is a story about a man named Elijah, who was a prophet of God. Elijah had displeased the king's wife and was very frightened. He ran away and ended up by hiding in a cave on Mount Sinai. Elijah longed for God to speak to him. Suddenly, Elijah knew that God wanted him to stand on top of the mountain. When he did so, a great wind shook the mountain, but Elijah could not hear God's voice in the wind. Then there was an earthquake, next a fire, but still God did not speak. Finally, there was a soft whisper and it was in the whisper that God spoke to Elijah. God is not always found where people expect him to be. (Story synopsis based on 1 Kings 19:1–13.)

Waiting for Fred

It was a windy October morning and a watery sun had at last pulled itself into the sky. Mrs Simpson put on her coat and her wellies and set off for the park. As usual, her dog, who answered to the name of Fred, was at her side. As soon as he was let off his lead, Fred disappeared, leaving Mrs Simpson to stroll along the path and enjoy the fresh air and autumn colours all around her.

Every so often she called out Fred's name and listened for a snuffle or a grunting noise just to make sure he was still there. Fred was chasing rabbits he would never catch and following smells that always disappeared. She found a tree stump and perched on the edge of it.

Today was so different from yesterday, when it had rained and she and Fred had got soaking wet. She scrunched her boots into the leaves on the ground around her, listening to the squelchy noise they made. Above her, the clouds were scudding across the deep blue sky and the tops of the trees swayed to and fro. This was the sort of day for flying kites and running across fields—a day to feel free, a day to enjoy being alive.

Mrs Simpson's favourite time of year had always been autumn. As a child, she had run through piles of dried leaves in the woods, kicking them up in the air and chasing them as they fell. Then she had gone home and curled up in the big chair by the fire in the front room. It was a funny memory to suddenly pop into her head.

She smiled as another memory flooded back—a memory of her teacher using the word 'current' to describe the wind. Mrs Simpson had gone home and asked her mother why currants, as in the things you eat, were in the sky being blown around— and why she couldn't see them.

She now knew that a currant with an 'a' was a dried grape and a current with an 'e' was when something was going by or through somewhere, like the wind or electricity or swirling water in the sea. You had to look at how the words were spelt to know which was which—'a' as in grape and 'e' as in electricity. Mrs Simpson had never got them confused again.

Her mother had also talked about God that day. She had said that, in some ways, God was like the wind because you could not actually see him—you just knew he was there. Whenever you saw anything that was beautiful, lovely or good, you knew God was there, in the same way that when you saw the light from an electric light bulb, you knew that a current was running through it.

She had also said that you could choose whether or not you wanted to be swept up and blown along by God. You could choose to ignore him because God didn't force himself on anyone. She had described a picture of a man knocking on a door with no handle. Only the person on the inside of the door could open it.

Mrs Simpson knew what she thought about the wind but was still not sure what she thought about God. Mrs Simpson had a friend who talked about God as though he was a friend. Her friend said she talked to God and he answered her prayers. Mrs Simpson had often wondered what it would be like to talk to God like that. Maybe she should find out more about it—but for now she had to find that dog of hers. She'd been sitting and thinking for rather a long time and he'd probably got his nose stuck down a rabbit hole by now.

'Fred!' she yelled.

Silence.

'Fred!' she tried once more. 'I am going home and if you don't come with me there will be no biscuits for…'

Fred appeared. The word 'biscuit' usually worked.

'Good boy!' Mrs Simpson said, taking his lead out of her pocket. 'Have you had a nice time out there with the rabbits?'

Fred shook himself but said nothing. Mrs Simpson laughed and, with Fred at her side, started for home. She thought of her big chair and bright fire. She looked up at the sky. The clouds were still scudding across, blown by invisible wind.

Things children have said

'… God is a spirit and you can't see him…'

'… he is a big, thoughtful beam of light…'

'… he sent Jesus to die for us on a cross because he wanted us to be friends with him…'

'… he loves me…'

'... he is like a cloud...'

'... he thinks about us all the time...'

'... I don't think he exists at all...'

'... he is everything and he loves me...'

'... he has got a son called Jesus who was born at Christmas time and died at Easter. They put him on a cross, but he came back to life again because he's dead strong...'

Thinking time for children

Think about whether or not you believe in God. Is it important to believe in him? Do you know anyone who does believe in him? What have they said about him? How could you get to know more about him?

Thinking time activity

Some people believe God exists, some don't. Think of three things you would want to say to someone who disagreed with you to help them understand what you believe.

Prayer

Dear God, there are lots of things we don't understand about you. Help us to understand more clearly. Amen

Valuing ourselves

Story summary

Helen buys a little wooden camel as a present for Simon and Lottie. The wooden camel knows he is loved by Helen, but is unsure about Simon and Lottie. They play roughly with him and he is surrounded by noise and hustle and bustle. The warm feeling he had when Helen looked after him disappears. It returns after Simon's fifth birthday party when the wooden camel is left outside and the children come out especially to find him. The story explores what it is like to know you are loved and valued with an unconditional love, just because you are you.

RE concept: Self-worth

 Exploring the concept

Children's understanding

- ○ Talk about how children know they are loved.
- ○ Talk about who loves them.
- ○ Talk about what it feels like to be loved and how this affects the way we see ourselves.

Religious overview

- ○ Discuss how faith communities value and show love to people.

Christian viewpoint

Christians believe that God created each person to be unique and that everyone is made in his image. God loved the people of this world so much, he was prepared to send his own Son to die for them. God does not love one person more than another. He loves everyone exactly the same with no favourites.

Do children agree with this viewpoint?

 Key Bible verse

'Even the hairs on your head are counted.'
MATTHEW 10:30

 Bible story link

In the Bible there is a story of a young boy named Joseph. He was sold by his brothers, taken to Egypt and later thrown into prison. Joseph's self-esteem must have been at rock bottom, yet he held on to his faith in God and knew that God had a purpose for his life. That purpose was to save many lives during a famine and then bring his family to safety to live in Egypt. (Story synopsis based on Genesis 37:1–36 and 39:1—47:12.)

The wooden camel

Helen and her mum went to the market. They ended up at a stall that sold carved wooden animals, and it was there that Helen first saw the little camel. There was something a bit special about him.

'That's what I want to get for Simon and Lottie,' she said.

Mum looked to where Helen was pointing and, a few minutes later, the camel and his cart were lowered into Helen's waiting arms.

'He's got such a sad face,' she said. 'Do you think I could make him smile?'

'I doubt it,' Mum said, without really thinking. 'We've got to wrap him up and send him to England tomorrow.'

Helen nodded. At least she had the rest of that day to try to make him smile.

She called the camel Charlie. He rather liked that, although, of course, he couldn't tell her. Neither could he tell her how proud he felt, taking her little pet mouse for rides on his cart. Helen pulled him so gently and he loved the feel of the mouse's soft fur on his wood. She dressed the camel up in a blue ribbon and kept him close by her for the rest of the day. A little happy feeling started to grow inside him. It spread down into his legs and across his smooth hump, for no other reason than because he knew he was loved.

'Charlie, smile for me,' Helen whispered.

But however hard he tried, he could not move his mouth. He was made of wood and his face would never change.

'Bye,' Helen whispered the following day. 'Thank you for letting me play with you and being my friend.' He did not know it but that was the last time he would ever hear Helen's voice.

Travelling halfway round the world covered in bubblewrap, brown paper and string was not something the wooden camel enjoyed. It was dark and hot and very uncomfortable. He was thrown about, dropped and had heavy things put on top of him. There were also strange, frightening noises that went on and on and on. How many times did he wish he were back with Helen? He lost count. All he knew was that the warm, happy feeling he had felt inside had disappeared.

Then the brown paper and bubblewrap were ripped off and light burned into the back of his eyes. Someone was reading the card that Helen's mum had put in the parcel.

'To Simon and Lottie. Hope you'll love this camel as much as Helen has done.'

The wooden camel found himself on a table in the middle of a room, and that was where he stayed. He had a new home, but it was not the same as Helen's.

The little wooden camel certainly never got bored, for there was always something going on. Simon and Lottie raced in and out, going here, there and everywhere, usually followed by their mum or dad. The camel had cars loaded on to his cart. He didn't always like that, because wheels dug into his wood and hurt him. Or he'd be sold when they played shops. He always seemed to be bought first and would find himself at the bottom of the shopping bag with other things shoved on top of him.

When the children were pretending to be doctors, his front legs were bandaged up. It reminded him of the time Helen had gently wrapped a ribbon round his neck, and he wished more than ever that he could have stayed with her. He remembered how she had loved him and the warm, happy feeling he'd had inside. All he felt now was empty and lonely and sad. 'Helen wanted me to smile,' he thought, 'but how can you if no one ever tells you how much you're loved?'

The wooden camel looked across at Teddy, who was sitting

on the other end of the table, dressed up in a tea towel and scarf. He was definitely loved. You could tell by the look on his face. It had a sort of smile on it all the time. Was it because he was soft and furry? The wooden camel could never be that.

Summer eventually gave way to autumn, which meant that Simon's fifth birthday was fast approaching. One evening, the children's mum sat down to write the invitations for Simon's birthday party. He was having a 'teddy bears' picnic' and seven of his friends were going to be invited. Simon became more and more excited about it and eventually the day arrived.

'If it doesn't rain, we'll eat outside,' Mum said as she started to get things ready. 'There'll be less mess for me to clear up afterwards.'

By five past two, everyone had arrived. The teddy bears were put on the table next to the wooden camel. The children played pass-the-parcel first, then hunt-the-picture. Dad had hidden 50 teddy bear pictures, which Mum had cut out of magazines, all over the house earlier in the day. Lottie found the most, partly because she had followed Dad round as he hid them, so she knew where they all were. After that, they watched a cartoon—about teddy bears, of course.

'We'll risk the weather and go outside to eat,' Mum said as the cartoon finished. 'At least I can see everyone through the window,' the wooden camel thought as he watched little hands grabbing their teddies. But someone picked him up, too, and he found himself on the edge of a blanket in the garden with the other teddies and the children. He was part of the party. They wanted him there. Someone even spilt their orange juice all over him. 'I don't mind,' he thought. 'It just makes me feel part of what's going on. It makes me feel loved.'

Just at that moment, it started to rain really hard.

'I don't believe it,' said Dad. 'Come on, everyone, inside!'

The children grabbed their teddies once more and raced towards the back door. Someone scooped up the blanket on which the wooden camel was lying. He felt his feet slipping. He was falling, falling. Down, down. His face hit the hard concrete of the patio as he fell and his cart crashed down on top of him. Then a small foot kicked him and he skidded into the fence.

At first he was not sure what had happened. There were noise and feet. Then the back door closed with a thud and there was nothing except the rain drumming on the concrete slab where he lay. He was wet and cold and his face hurt where he had fallen.

'I can't cry,' he thought, 'because I'm made out of wood, but the raindrops are my tears. I'm crying for you, Helen. You wanted me to smile, but I know I never will because they don't love me. They didn't really want me at their party. I was brought out by mistake and they haven't even noticed I'm missing.'

He lay there for a long, long time. Darkness crept over the garden and a chill wind set in. He heard the children leave as the party ended and watched as the blinds were pulled down at the kitchen window. It was going to be a long, dark night.

Suddenly the back door was thrown open and Simon burst into the garden. 'I'm not going to bed until I've found him,' he announced. 'He's one of my most favourite toys and I don't care if I get wet. I'm going to look for him.'

'He must have lost his teddy,' the wooden camel thought. 'I didn't know there was someone else out here as well as me, getting soaked in the rain.' Then he brightened up. Maybe they would find him while they were looking for the teddy.

Lottie came out with Dad. He had a torch and an umbrella and moved slowly across the garden, swinging the beam of light from side to side. The wooden camel winced as the light fell on his face.

'Found him,' Dad called out.

'Oh no,' he said. 'A bit of wood's broken off his mouth. It must have happened when he was dropped.'

The wooden camel felt himself being picked up and put

into Simon's waiting arms—just like the first time Helen had held him, by the stall in the market. Her arms had been gentle and she had wanted to look after him. Simon's arms were like that now, and what was it Simon had said a few minutes ago about looking for one of his favourite toys? He must have been talking about…

The wooden camel looked up at Simon's face. Simon smiled down at him. And in that moment a warm, happy feeling, like the one he had lost so long ago, started to grow in the camel's tummy. It spread all over him—just like when you know you are loved.

'See where that bit of wood's chipped off his mouth,' Dad said, as they took him inside. 'It almost looks as if he's smiling now.'

Simon looked closely at the precious toy in his arms, and the rather special little wooden camel simply smiled back at him.

Things children have said

'… sometimes someone thinks about you and after a bit they stop. But I still love him even if he doesn't come and see me any more…'

'… everyone is important to someone…'

'… they give you presents when you go to see them…'

'… they could tell you they love you. That's best…'

'… they listen to you when you want to tell them something…'

'... my mum gave my dad a card on Valentine's day last year and it was dead soppy...'

'... my mum gives me kisses...'

'... it's nice to know someone loves you. My mum tells me sometimes. My brother doesn't, but I don't like him anyway...'

Thinking time for children

Think of one person you love. How do you show that you love them? How do other people show that they love you? What does it feel like to be loved? If you were to say one thing about each person in this room that showed why you liked being with them, what would it be?

Thinking time activity

Draw a picture of yourself and round it draw ten things you are really good at doing.

Prayer

Dear God, thank you that it does not matter what we look like, or where we live, or what clothes we wear, or how we speak, or who our friends are, or where we were born. Thank you that you love us for who we are. Help us to love other people in the way that you love us.
Amen

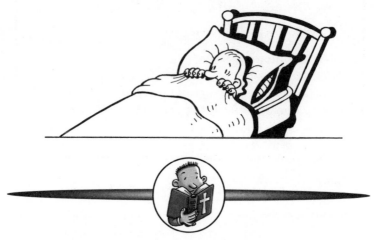

Being scared
is OK

Story summary

The following poem deals with things that frighten people. The material encourages children to be completely honest about what is frightening and what isn't. The poem was written in conjunction with a Year 3 class and models the way children think about scary things.

RE concept: Honesty

 Exploring the concept

Children's understanding

- Talk about what being honest means and its consequences, particularly in the light of trust being built on honesty.
- Discuss whether being totally honest is easy or difficult.
- Explore examples of when children have been honest even when it was hard.

Religious overview

- Explore rules and guidelines in different faith communities about being honest.

Christian viewpoint

Christians believe that honesty and trust go hand in hand. In the Bible, God is described as completely trustworthy and early Christians tried to model such trustworthiness in their own lives, based not only on God's promises in the scriptures but also on the example Jesus gave in his own life and teaching. Christian faith has always been built on trust.

Do children agree with this viewpoint?

 Key Bible verse

We can be proud of our clear conscience. We have always lived honestly and sincerely... And we were guided by God's wonderful kindness instead of by the wisdom of this world.

2 CORINTHIANS 1:12

Bible story link

There are many stories of people in the Bible who overcame fear because they trusted in God. One such person was Moses, who was given the task of leading the people of Israel out of captivity in Egypt. Moses didn't feel up to the task and tried to wriggle out of what God was asking him to do. But finally, after repeatedly facing the wrath and stubbornness of the king of Egypt, Moses helped his people to flee from Egypt. With God's help, he led them through the parted waters of the Red Sea and into the desert lands of the Sinai Peninsula. The journey across the desert lasted many years and was often dangerous. (Story synopsis based on Exodus 4:1—14:31.)

I'm scared

Sometimes I'm scared
When I lie in my bed
On my own in the dark.

Why?

Because sometimes
My head is full of things
I don't like to think about.

Am I ever going to get to sleep?
Or will I lie here, wide awake,
And scared all night?

Where's my teddy?

I wish I were older.

Then I'd stay up longer.
But I have to go to bed

And in my head are
Scary things I've seen on TV,
Scary things I've seen in books.
Something someone said to me,
Scary words and scary looks.

Sometimes I don't understand
And sometimes I feel silly
Because I should have known
What they were talking about.
Only I didn't.

'Try to get to sleep,' says Mum
When I tell her.
Only she doesn't remember
What it's like to be little
In a great big world.

In my head are narrow pavements
With gi-normous lorries rumbling by
And the horrid, smelly dog that barks
Behind the big black gate
That we have to walk past
On the way to school.

And I don't like it
Because one day,
That
Dog
Might
Jump over the gate
And get me.

There are loads of other things
Which I'm trying not to think about
And I want to go to sleep,

But

I don't want any nightmares.
That's why I'm scared
When I lie in my bed
On my own, in the dark.

Am I ever going to get to sleep?

Things children have said

About the dark

'... I don't like the shadows my night light makes...'

'... there's a door to our loft outside my bedroom door and I think there's a nasty man up there with a knife and he wants to get me...'

'... if I need a toilet in the middle of the night and I have to go downstairs, I always think there's a robber in our sitting room and he's going to get me as I go past the door. I run dead quick until I get there...'

'... if I'm on the top bunk, I'm scared I'll fall out and hurt myself. I did once and my mum got cross with me...'

'... you don't know what's going on in the dark. It might be nasty. You just don't know...'

'... kidnappers come out at night and might take me away and hurt me...'

'... we go shopping in the dark sometimes and I have to hold on to the buggy and walk next to the bushes. I always think someone's going to jump out of the bushes and get me, and my mum will look after the baby and leave me alone...'

About bathrooms

'... I used to think there was a monster who lived down the toilet and he would come up and bite my bottom if I sat on it too long...'

'... when you turn on our taps in the bathroom, the water squirts all over the place and that scares me...'

'... my nanny gets spiders in her bath. I always have a shower when I'm there...'

'... we have a fan that comes on in our bathroom and I think it looks at me as it goes round...'

About things seen on screens

'... my mum doesn't always let me watch the things she does. She says they'll scare me...'

'... I thought there was an alien with green eyes in my bedroom after I watched a film once. My mum told me to stop being so stupid, but she hadn't seen the film because I watched it at Kevin's house...'

'... I imagined there was zombies sucking blood out of my neck because that's what they do on my new computer game. I didn't tell my mum or dad because they would have taken the game away from me, and I still wanted to play it even though it scared me...'

About cupboards

'... the door creaks when you open it...'

'... our airing cupboard scares me because it's got a big red thing inside it that makes all funny noises. I hear it when I'm trying to go to sleep. I think it might explode and pour boiling hot water all over me...'

About parents

'... when he gets cross I get really scared in case he starts throwing things at me...'

'... my mum says she's going to the sitting room when I'm trying to go to sleep. But I know she's not because I hear her in the kitchen. She's told me a lie and she shouldn't do that...'

About robbers

'... my friend's house had robbers and I thought it might happen to us...'

'... if a robber came in my house, he might wear a mask, and I don't like people wearing masks because you can't see their faces and they might hurt me...'

About the wind

'... it's stronger than me. It might knock me over and I'd hurt myself...'

About people

'... if my friends break up with me, I have no one to protect me in the playground...'

'... when they're bigger than me and I know they're going to be nasty to me even though I've told my mummy about them...'

Thinking time for children

Often, the first step to making things that scare us go away is to tell someone about them. Is there something or someone who scares you at the moment? Who could you tell? When could you tell them? What would you say?

Thinking time activity

Draw a picture of the things you are scared of. Do you think you will always be scared of them? Is your friend scared of the same things?

Prayer

Dear God, help me remember that you are always with me wherever I go. Amen

Boredom

Story summary

Spencer has to go to a fund-raising fashion show with his mother. He expects it to be boring and so it is until he is asked to hand out plates of food and become involved. The story looks at how taking part and 'owning' something makes it much more interesting.

RE concept: Ownership

 Exploring the concept

Children's understanding
❂ Talk about what it means to own something and look after it.

Religious overview
❂ Explore how people practise their faith by attending worship, studying scriptures and meeting with other believers.
❂ Talk about how this gives people an identity and ownership of their faith.

Christian viewpoint
Christians believe that, through baptism, they become part of God's family and belong to each other because they belong to God.

Do children agree with this viewpoint?

 Key Bible verses

All of you are part of the same body. There is only one Spirit of God, just as you were given one hope when you were chosen to be God's people. We have only one Lord, one faith, and one baptism. There is one God who is the Father of all people. Not only is God above all others, but he works by using all of us, and he lives in all of us.

EPHESIANS 4:4–6

 Bible story link

After Jesus died, rose again and went back to heaven, the first disciples began to live their lives as he had taught them. The Bible says that they often met together and they shared everything they had. They met in each other's homes to worship God together and shared their food happily and freely. They owned their faith and committed themselves to it. (Story synopsis based on Acts 2:44.)

Do I have to go?

'Do I have to?' Spencer groaned.

'Marie can't babysit, so yes, you do.'

'Mum, it's Friday night and I want to watch television, not go to a boring old fashion show.'

'We'll be home by half past nine and it's at your old infant school, so you can have a look round while you're there. You'll enjoy that.'

'But, Mum, boys don't go to fashion shows.'

'My boy does.'

It was no good. Mum was going, Spencer was going, and that was that.

Spencer was surprised to see his class photograph from four years ago still up in the school entrance hall. There he was, still smiling on the back row next to Charlie Millar. The floor tiles were the same green, but the secretary's door was now painted bright blue. It had been red before. Everything seemed so much smaller, though, especially the main hall.

The din of high-pitched voices greeted them as they entered the hall. There was a line of stage blocks, covered with dark yellow material, dividing the hall in two.

'They're for the models to walk along,' Mum said. 'If you go to a proper fashion show it's called a catwalk.'

Mum was looking round for her friends. They had not yet arrived.

'Look, there's Mrs Marston,' Mum said, to pass the time. 'Let's go and say "hello" to her.'

Mrs Marston had been Spencer's teacher when he was in Year 1.

'My goodness me, it's Spencer,' she said. 'Haven't you grown?'

'Aren't children supposed to grow?' Spencer thought as he smiled sweetly.

'What year is he in now?' Mrs Marston asked Mum.

'Year 5. He's ten next month,' Mum said. 'But he's still my little boy, aren't you, Spency-pops?'

Spencer gasped. How dare she use that pet name in public, and in front of a teacher as well!

'Well, I'm in charge of the food,' Mrs Marston said, 'so I'd better hurry along and make sure everything's all right.'

'I didn't know there was food,' Spencer said as she disappeared. Maybe coming here wouldn't be so awful after all.

'It's only finger food, but it's better than nothing,' Mum smiled. She glanced at the hall door. Two of her friends were standing there.

'Coo-ee,' she called out and waved at them. They waved back.

'Am I really here?' Spencer cringed. He hung his head and trailed across the hall after her. All those chair legs scraping and women laughing in squeaky voices—it was getting on his nerves.

'I had to bring Spencer with me,' Mum announced to her friends. 'The babysitter's ill.'

Spencer sat on the chair next to her. He swung his legs and scraped the floor with the soles of his shoes.

'Stop doing that,' Mum said, in between telling Lucy about the postman delivering the wrong letters to their house for the third day running.

'I'm bored,' he whispered.

'Well, go and ask Mrs Marston if you can help with the food. That'll give you something to do.'

'What an excellent idea,' Mrs Marston said. 'Take one of these plates to each of the tables and make sure you go round the stage blocks. You might hurt yourself if you try to scramble over them.'

'OK,' he said and picked up a plate laden with little cakes, slices of quiche, sandwiches, bits of pizza, sausages on sticks and several things he did not recognize. Maybe life was not so boring after all.

Before long, a girl joined him. She was in the year above him at school. 'Can I help, too?' she asked.

'Of course you can, my dear,' Mrs Marston said, 'but mind the stage blocks. I don't want you hurting yourself.'

'Well, *I'm* going to climb over the stage blocks,' Rebecca whispered. 'It's a long way round otherwise and these plates are heavy.'

'Mrs Marston said we were to…'

'I don't care,' Rebecca cut in. 'I didn't want to come tonight but my mum made me, so I'm going to do what I like.'

And with that, she climbed up on to the stage blocks, ducking down so no one would notice her. The plate of food she was carrying tipped forward and a slice of mushroom quiche landed on the dark yellow material covering the catwalk.

'I should pick that up,' Spencer thought. 'I really ought to, but I can't be bothered.' He wasn't normally a naughty boy but, like Rebecca, he did not really want to be there. He was bored and a bit angry, so he walked away and left the slice of mushroom quiche where it had fallen.

Eventually, the lady who was organizing the evening stood up and coughed very loudly. She thanked everyone for coming and said the fashion show would start in two minutes. Spencer and Rebecca settled themselves on little chairs next to the stage blocks. If they had got to be there, at least they would make sure they had a good view. The hall lights dimmed and floodlights aimed at the stage blocks came on.

'Welcome to Starson's fashion show,' a new voice drooled into the microphone. 'All the clothes being modelled tonight can be bought from Starson's Superstore in town. We look forward to seeing you there in the near future.'

'Not likely,' Spencer thought as the first model drifted across the stage blocks. 'That dress is revolting.' The dress in question was black, covered with green sequins, and cost £499. Phew! There was no way Mum would spend that much on a dress.

The next outfit had a huge hole in the side of it. Apparently, it had come from Paris. Spencer thought it was horrible, too. He tried to think how he could make the next few minutes more interesting. He found a big scab on his elbow where he had fallen over in the playground. If he wiggled his fingernail under the edge, it might come off.

Rebecca suddenly leaned towards him.

'Did you drop some food on the stage blocks?' she whispered.

'No,' he whispered back, 'you did.'

There, in the middle of the third stage block down, was the slice of mushroom quiche, waiting for one of the unsuspecting models to tread on it. Spencer held his breath as a fake leopardskin trouser suit strutted towards it.

'Go on, get it,' he breathed.

The fake leopardskin trouser suit missed by three centimetres. They watched in fascination as high heels passed before them, each time narrowly missing the slice of squidgy, squashy mushroom quiche begging to be trodden on.

It was the green knitted dress, priced at £450, that shot sideways and disappeared over the side of the stage blocks. Quite impressive, really. It gave a little scream as it went.

Everyone gasped and leaned forward. The model un-wrapped her arms and legs from the owner of the chair she had fallen on top of, and stood up. Spencer and Rebecca looked at each other. Then they looked at what was left of the mushroom quiche.

Rebecca started giggling. So did Spencer. The voice boomed into the microphone.

'We'll take a short break. Katrina is one of our favourite models and we do need to make sure she is all right.'

The main hall lights were turned on and several people attacked the stage blocks with dustpans and brushes. Spencer and Rebecca decided to return to their mothers, who were talking about the fallen model. 'She slipped. Now can we go home?' Spencer thought. But no, the hall lights were dimmed once more and the floodlights turned on. Spencer tried, unsuccessfully, to fall asleep. It was not as if his mother was going to buy any of the clothes.

'Can we go home now?' he asked as soon as it was all over.

'OK,' Mum sighed and began putting her coat on.

'Did you enjoy any of it?' she asked as they walked along the road together.

'Only when that model fell off the stage blocks,' Spencer said. 'And giving out the food was just about all right.'

'Did you see what she slipped on?' Mum asked. 'You were at the front.'

'Um... her shoe got stuck on something, I think,' Spencer said.

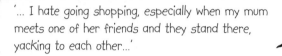

Things children have said

'... I hate going shopping, especially when my mum meets one of her friends and they stand there, yacking to each other...'

'... having to watch my brother's television programmes...'

'... long aeroplane journeys. You're meant to enjoy them because you're going on holiday...'

'... being told to go to sleep...'

'... going in the car to see my gran...'

'... I hate going to garden centres...'

'... the park, because I have no brothers or sisters and Mum expects me to play on my own...'

'... tests in school, they are so boring...'

'... Spencer started to enjoy himself when he wasn't just sitting down but had something to do...'

'... when I get bored I twirl my hair, bite my nails, bite my lip and then my mum tells me off... I sigh loudly, complain, annoy my little brother, then wait for Mum or Dad to come and tell him off. That's good fun, that is...'

'... imagine I'm somewhere else, doing something I want to do. It's hard sometimes but that's what I try and do...'

> '... being bored makes me just want to do something even if it's naughty...'
>
> '... you want to get your own back on your mum for taking you somewhere where it's boring...'

Thinking time for children

What is the most boring thing you ever have to do? Why? What is the most interesting? Why? Is there anything you can do to make the boring things become interesting? What do you do when you get bored? Does this ever get you into trouble? How can you tell someone in a nice way that what they do bores you? Is it right to tell them?

Thinking time activity

Draw a grid—for example, three squares by four—and mark in each box things you did yesterday. Colour the interesting ones in blue, the boring ones in red and the ones in between in yellow. Did you 'own' any of them and get involved in what was happening? Put dots on the ones you owned—the more you owned it, the more dots.

See if there is a link between the blue squares and those with the most number of dots.

Prayer

Dear God, thank you for all the interesting things I do. Thank you for all the interesting people I meet and spend time with. Amen

Owning up

Story summary

When the yo-yo man comes to school, his special rattlesnake yo-yo goes missing. Joshua knows that Pete took it but, when asked, pretends he knows nothing about it. In the end, Joshua does own up and the reader is asked what his punishment should be for not being honest and owning up in the first place. The story looks at issues of honesty and owning up when something wrong has been done.

RE concept:
Punishment and forgiveness

 ## Exploring the concept

Children's understanding

- Talk about the punishments children think should be given for various offences.
- Discuss why these punishments should be handed out.
- Talk about who should decide on the punishments and enforce them.
- Discuss whether punishment and forgiveness should go together.

Religious overview

- Explore what different religions have to say about punishment and forgiveness.

Christian viewpoint

Christians believe that, through Jesus, they have been forgiven for the things they say, do and think that are wrong. However, this does not mean they can do wrong things without consequence. God wants people to be the best they can be, and that means owning up when they do wrong things and taking responsibility for their actions. Christians believe that God corrects them when they do wrong because he loves them.

Do children agree with this viewpoint?

 ## Key Bible verses

If we say that we have not sinned, we are fooling ourselves, and the truth isn't in our hearts. But if we confess our sins to God, he can always be trusted to forgive us and take our sins away.

1 JOHN 1:8–9

The Lord corrects the people he loves and disciplines those he calls his own.

HEBREWS 12:6

Bible story link

One day, Jesus' close friend, Peter, asked him how many times we should forgive someone who has done us wrong. Was seven times enough? Jesus answered that we should forgive them 77 times—that is to say, more times than we can count! He went on to tell the story of a servant who owed a huge amount of money to the king. The king let him off the debt. Immediately, the servant went out and threw a fellow servant into jail because of a small debt he owed him. When the king heard what had happened, he was very angry and had the first servant severely punished because he had not learnt the lesson to forgive others as we are forgiven. (Story synopsis based on Matthew 18:21–34.)

The yo-yo man

At lunchtime, Mr Johnston asked Joshua and Pete to get the hall ready.

'Has the yo-yo man arrived?' Joshua asked.

The head teacher nodded.

'I can't wait for this!' Pete grinned.

'Look,' he whispered as they entered the hall. 'The yo-yos are out already.'

The two boys admired the contents of about 15 boxes that were laid out on a table. Pete suddenly picked up one of the yo-yos and slipped the loop over his middle finger. The sparkly green yo-yo rattled as it dropped towards the floor.

'Whoooo!' he hissed. 'That's some yo-yo. Did you hear the sound it made?'

'Come on,' Joshua said, 'we shouldn't be touching them.'

'It doesn't matter,' Pete said. He took the loop off his finger and put the yo-yo in his pocket. Just like that. He stole it.

'You're not going to keep it, are you?' Joshua asked.

Pete nodded.

'The yo-yo man's got loads of them. He works for a company that makes them. He can get another one if he wants to.'

'But he'll tell Mr Johnston and Mr Johnston will know it's us,' Joshua argued back.

'He won't,' Pete said, 'because we're not going to say anything about it. Are we?'

And with that, he counted the chairs down the side of the hall to make sure there were enough for the teachers to sit on and walked towards the hall door.

Joshua felt a bit sick inside his stomach. What should he do now? Pete had gone, leaving him to put out the benches and chairs. Even worse, Pete still had the yo-yo with him.

Half an hour later, the whole school was in the hall, staring at the yo-yo man in his luminous green waistcoat and special black gloves, which only covered his index and middle fingers. He was doing a stunt, sending two black yo-yos in different directions. They were so fast, but they never hit each other. Joshua looked across at Pete, who was sitting at the other end of the bench. He was smiling, a secret sort of smile.

Next the yo-yo man showed off his red, blue, purple and transparent cruiser yo-yo. He span a spotty pink triple-play round and round, 'walked the dog' with a grey one, 'rocked the baby' with a yellow one and 'looped the loop' with a huge black one. He made the outlines of three-leafed clovers, bow ties and rolls of spaghetti. He told jokes and made the whole school laugh. Joshua should have enjoyed it, but he didn't.

'Always make sure you have enough space to play safely,' the yo-yo man said, 'and remember, practice makes perfect. Don't give up if you can't do something straight away.'

He stooped down by one of the Year 3s.

'And how old are you?' he asked.

'Seven,' a little voice replied.

'I was seven when I was your age,' he said, and everyone laughed again.

'The hitch makes the yo-yo come back up the string. It's three wraps round the axle. Now somewhere I've got my rattlesnake.' He turned his back on them and went to his table.

Everyone waited. Joshua held his breath as the yo-yo man picked up an empty yo-yo box and put it back down again. Then he checked in his bag.

'It seems I didn't bring my special rattlesnake yo-yo with me, so I can't do my last trick.'

There was a murmur of disappointment. 'So I'll just say, always do your best, never give up and thank you very much, you've been a wonderful audience.'

Everyone clapped and cheered. Mr Johnston thanked him for coming and reminded them that yo-yos would be on sale in the library at the end of the day. While the Year 3s were leaving the hall, the yo-yo man spoke to Mr Johnston. Then Mr Johnston walked over to the Year 6 children.

'Pete, Joshua, can I have a word, please?'

Joshua gulped. His knees trembled slightly as he stood up.

'I know you wouldn't have touched any of the yo-yos because you're far too sensible,' Mr Johnston said, 'but did you see anyone come in here when you were getting the chairs and benches out?'

'There were some Year 5s hanging around outside,' Pete said.

'Who?' Mr Johnston asked.

'Can't remember,' Pete said.

'Well, if you do remember, can you let me know?'

And with that, he left them. Pete caught Joshua's eye. It looked as if they had got away with it.

'Told you it would be all right, didn't I?' Pete whispered.

That night, though, Joshua could not sleep. His mind kept thinking about what Pete had done, and he knew Pete was wrong. He should not have taken that yo-yo, and Joshua was wrong because he hadn't said anything to Mr Johnston.

The next day, everyone took their yo-yos into school. They were not normally allowed to take them in, but today was different. Several extra teachers were on playground duty and chatted to the children as they tried not to hit each other. Mr Johnston wandered over to where Joshua was trying to master 'walking the dog' without much success.

'Did you enjoy the yo-yo man's visit?' he asked.

Joshua nodded.

'Joshua, I am going to ask you something and I want you to be absolutely honest with me. When you and Pete were in the hall setting up yesterday, did you touch any of the yo-yos?'

Joshua paused. It had been Pete who had actually touched them, not him. He looked at Mr Johnston.

'No,' he said.

'Are you sure?'

'I did not touch any of the yo-yos,' Joshua said.

'Did you see anyone else touch them?'

Joshua paused for a second. When he was eating his breakfast that morning, he had not seen anyone touching any yo-yos. So if Mr Johnston was asking him about then, the answer was simple.

'No,' he said. He felt his face flushing as he said it.

'Joshua,' Mr Johnston said in a gentle voice, 'I'm going to ask you one more time. Do you know anything about the yo-yo going missing?'

Joshua looked at the ground. Then he took a deep, deep breath.

'Pete put it in his pocket,' he whispered.

'Thank you,' Mr Johnston said, 'for being honest at last. The yo-yo man was only out of the hall for five minutes. He saw you and Pete going in and saw you coming out, separately. It had to be one of you.'

'Sorry,' Joshua said. He was tired.

'You didn't sleep very well last night, did you?' the head teacher said.

Joshua shook his head.

'I kept thinking about the yo-yo,' he said.

Mr Johnston sighed. 'I want you to stay here,' he said, 'while I have a chat with Pete, and I really hope you both learn a lesson from this.'

Things children have said

'... Mr Johnston was sensible to talk to Joshua and Pete on their own because he does not want rumours to start and have people exaggerating what has happened...'

'... you might own up better if you're on your own....'

'... stay inside all of dinnertime to think about what he has done...'

'... I'd make Pete and Joshua miss playtime and have extra homework and tell their parents and get them to punish them as well...'

'... they spoiled the yo-yo man's show for everyone...'

'... I'd make him pay for the yo-yo and say sorry to the yo-yo man and be told off in front of the whole school...'

'... other children need to know they can't go round stealing things, especially if a visitor has come to the school...'

'... I'd punish them to stop them doing it again and because they let the school down...'

'... lying and stealing is always wrong...'

'... not owning up if you have done something wrong is as bad as lying and cheating...'

'... being honest and owning up all the time is very hard...'

'... I'd have told Pete to put the yo-yo back or I wouldn't be his friend...'

'... threaten to tell on him if he didn't put it back...'

'... tell a teacher but ask the teacher not to tell Pete it was me who had told on him...'

'... walk away and go to play with someone else or else try to persuade him to put it back...'

'... Joshua didn't enjoy what he should have enjoyed because of what Pete did...'

'... if you get found out when you are stealing, you will lie...'

'... you lie if you're going to get the blame for something, so it's to get out of trouble...'

'... you can lie without stealing but you can't steal without lying. One leads to the other, well it does usually...'

Thinking time for children

Think about a time when you have been punished. What did you learn from it? Was it a fair punishment? What is the biggest thing you have ever forgiven someone? What's the biggest thing you have ever been forgiven yourself? What punishment should Pete and Joshua be given? Why?

Thinking time activity

Draw a circle and, inside it, write down a lie you might be tempted to tell. Round the outside of the circle, write down all the people who might be affected by that lie. Now think whether those people might want to punish you or forgive you if they found out about your lie. Why?

Prayer

Dear God, it seems easy to tell lies sometimes. Help me to be really brave and always tell the truth. If someone asks me to tell a lie for them, please help me to find a way so that I can always tell the whole truth. Amen

Anger

Story summary

Chrissie's mum's car is wheel-clamped when she parks it on a piece of waste ground near the shops. The wheel clampers are threatening and unpleasant and make Mum feel powerless and angry. The anger spills over to the rest of the day and affects other people. The story explores how anger can be expressed (and should be expressed) safely and looks at how anger affects others.

RE concept: Anger

 Exploring the concept

Children's understanding

- Talk about when children have been angry, what caused the anger and how they dealt with it.
- Discuss how anger has consequences if it isn't handled properly.
- Explore whether children think anger is a good thing or bad.

Religious overview

- Explore how anger is viewed by people who have a religious faith.
- Discuss whether this is the same for those without faith.

Christian viewpoint

Christians believe that, in certain circumstances, it is right for people to be angry. However, anger should always be constructive, never destructive and never out of control.

Do children agree with this viewpoint?

 Key Bible verse

Don't get so angry that you sin. Don't go to bed angry.
EPHESIANS 4:26

 Bible story link

One day, Jesus went to the temple in Jerusalem and was appalled to see money changers and tradesmen cheating as they sold cattle, sheep and pigeons for people to use as offerings and sacrifices to God. He made a whip and drove everyone out of the temple forecourts. He overturned tables and scattered money on the floor, telling people to stop making his Father's house a market place and den of thieves.

Jesus was angry and expressed it. He was angry because the temple, which was meant for people to worship God, was now being used for people to make money out of worshippers. (Story synopsis based on John 2:13–22.)

The clampers

Chrissie was scared—so scared, she hardly knew what to do. Mum was angry—so angry, Chrissie thought she was going to explode. And it was all because Mum had driven to the shops and left the car in the little road where she always left it.

They had bought a comic, a tin of dog food and a carton of cream from the little shop on the corner. That was all. It had taken them no longer than three minutes. But, as they returned to the car, they saw a very tall, very strong-looking man with a black eye, leaning against the door of their car.

'Excuse me,' Mum said. 'Why are you leaning against my car?'

'Because, Madam, you've been clamped,' he muttered.

'I've been what?'

'Clamped.'

A bright yellow chunk of metal had been attached to the front wheel of Mum's car. The man kicked it as he stood up straight. He now towered over Mum, who took a step backwards.

'Why have you done that?' she asked.

The man waved towards three little signs on the wall on the other side of the road.

'If you can read,' he said sarcastically, 'you will know that wheel-clamping is in operation. That'll be £125 if you want your car back.'

'I don't believe this,' Mum said. 'I've parked here for years and no one's ever said anything before.'

'Well, it's changed now. You should have read the signs before you parked, and if I don't get £125, I don't undo the clamp.'

He tossed the key to the clamp in the air, caught it and put it in his pocket. Chrissie looked at the huge scar running down the side of his face, the hole where one of his front teeth was missing and his black eye, which twitched when he spoke.

'I'm a bouncer in a nightclub when I'm not doing this,' he commented, folding his arms across his chest, 'and this is my mate, Kev.'

From behind a van parked next to their car, another man appeared. He was even bigger and uglier than the first and was clutching a long metal bar in his hand.

'Is the lady refusing to pay for parking where she shouldn't have?' Kev asked.

Mum opened her purse.

'Hurry up,' Kev said. 'We haven't got all day.'

'And I haven't got £125,' Mum said. There was a quiver in her voice. Even she was a bit rattled by Kev's appearance.

'The bank's just round the corner,' the first clamper said. 'We're leaving in ten minutes and if we haven't had £125 from you by then, we take your car with us. Then it will cost you an extra £150 per day to get it back.'

Mum grabbed Chrissie's hand and stormed her way towards the bank. Chrissie had to run to keep up with her.

'I'll... I'll...' Mum began once they were round the corner. She wasn't just angry. She was livid, with pure white-hot rage.

They reached the hole in the wall outside the bank.

'Can I do it?' Chrissie asked.

'If you must,' Mum said, and handed Chrissie the card.

Chrissie punched in the PIN. She knew it by heart and had kept her promise never to tell anyone what it was.

'How much shall I get out?' she asked.

'I don't know. How much did those stupid little men want?'

'£125.'

'Get £200 then. I need some for next week.'

Chrissie pressed what she thought were the right numbers, then waited. One £20 note appeared.

'You silly girl, can't I trust you to do anything right?'

'I thought I'd pushed the right ones,' Chrissie whispered.

'Well, you didn't, did you?' Mum almost screamed. 'Here, let me do it.'

Chrissie moved back from the machine and clutched her comic. She wished she had stayed at home. She did not like her mum when she was like this.

'Right. Let's go and pay those men,' Mum hissed 30 seconds later, 'then I'm going to phone the police and I'm going to write a letter to the council and the local newspaper and our MP and demand they do something about it.'

'Well, you won't be parking here again, will you?' the first clamper said as he folded the notes and slid them into his back pocket. 'It's a good site, this, we're making over £6000 a day. And don't bother going to the police. They've checked us out already and they're fed up with people like you phoning them.'

Mum didn't say anything. She and Chrissie watched as the clamp was taken off the front wheel.

'In,' she muttered to Chrissie.

Chrissie got in. So did Mum. She turned the key and revved up the engine. She wanted to drive off in style, but instead she stalled the car. The first clamper and Kev stood there laughing at her.

Chrissie's mum swore—two very rude words. Chrissie decided not to say anything in case the same words were directed at her.

'Lie low,' Chrissie said to Thumper when they got home. 'Mum's not happy, but she's got some friends coming round later and has got to do some cooking, so as long as neither of us goes in the kitchen we'll be all right.'

Thumper wagged his tail and lay down by the window in the front room. Sensible dog.

The rice boiled over and made a mess on the hob, the chicken wouldn't cook properly and the pudding would not defrost fast enough. Apart from that, everything was fine, and Mum's two friends arrived at half past seven. As soon as they came through the front door, Mum started to tell them about the clampers.

Chrissie retreated upstairs and Thumper went with her. Half an hour later, food was served. Thumper joined them. He always did.

'Ever hopeful, aren't you?' Chrissie whispered. Thumper wagged his tail and sniffed round Mum's friends. They were still talking about wheel-clamping. Juliette knew someone who had been clamped in Portugal, and Diane's neighbour, the one with the false teeth and dyed hair, had been clamped last year in London.

Then it happened. Mum slopped a tiny piece (and it was only a tiny piece) of chicken on the floor. Thumper shot across the room to get it, headbutting Diane's feet as he did so. Diane was not used to dogs throwing themselves at her feet and she screamed. Somehow her plate ended up on the floor and Thumper, unable to believe his good fortune, stuck his nose in it and began slurping and wagging his tail.

'Out!' Mum screamed at him and grabbed hold of his collar. 'I've had enough of you.'

'I'm so sorry,' she said as she came back into the dining room.

Chrissie felt sorry for Thumper. All he'd done was pretend to be a vacuum cleaner. He had not meant to hurt Diane's feet, but now there was the carpet to mop up and more fussing.

Fortunately, Mum had made plenty of food. She gave Diane another plate.

'Now, Chrissie, have you nearly finished?' Mum asked a few minutes later.

Chrissie knew that was the signal for her to go. Mum and her friends chatted about boring things in more detail when she was not there. She'd be called when it was time for pudding—or dessert, as Mum called it when she had friends to supper. Strawberry pavlova and lemon meringue pie were on the menu tonight.

Well, they would have been if Thumper hadn't found them first. Their sorry state showed how much he had enjoyed nosing his way through them, like a digger making a trench.

'Bad dog,' Chrissie snapped, and hit him on the nose. Normally she would never have done that, but somehow tonight was different. Tonight, everyone was cross with everyone else. Thumper made a rapid sideways move and Mum's favourite vase, which was on the kitchen table, crashed to the floor and broke.

'Chrissie, I don't care if it's an hour before your usual bedtime, you're going to bed!' Mum said from the doorway, 'And you, Thumper, are going outside in the garden.'

'Mum, that's not fair!' Chrissie began, but got no further. It was pointless arguing with Mum when she was in a mood like this. She would never listen. It was easier to do as she said and go to bed. No strawberry pavlova, no lemon meringue pie, no cream, no watching television, no reading her comic—and it all started with the wheel clamper.

Chrissie held her teddy bear very tightly and wondered if he was feeling as unhappy as she was. Then she wondered how Thumper was feeling. He was outside in the garden in the pouring rain.

It was nearly midnight when Juliette and Diane left. Chrissie woke up as the front door closed. A little while later, Mum tiptoed upstairs.

'Are you still awake?' she whispered as she knelt beside the bed. Chrissie turned her head towards her.

'I'm sorry I was cross with you earlier. I was so angry, but I shouldn't have taken it out on you.'

Chrissie opened her eyes.

'I'm sorry,' Mum said again.

'Is Thumper still outside?' Chrissie asked.

'No. I let him in. Was I nasty to him, too?'

Chrissie nodded. Her mum was back to normal again.

'I told him I'd take him for an extra long walk tomorrow to make up for it.'

It wasn't Thumper's fault Mum had been wheel-clamped. Neither was it Chrissie's.

'New day tomorrow,' Mum said, 'and I'm not going to get wheel-clamped.'

'I'm glad about that,' Chrissie said.

Things children have said

'... I'm glad Mum calmed down...'

'... you might not know everything before you get cross. Then it's wrong...'

'... it's all right to get angry as long as you don't hurt anyone or say anything you don't really mean...'

'... when you're cross you can say things you wish you hadn't said afterwards...'

235

'... I don't like it when people get cross with me...'

'... when someone's angry with me, I get very scared and upset...'

'... terrified they'll hit me and hurt me...'

'... my nan got angry with my mum when she tried to help her with her bills... Nan didn't understand...'

'... most adults change when they get angry...'

'... it's when they get upset or are in a hurry and we're not...'

'... they say things they don't mean afterwards...'

'... I hate it when my dad comes in and he's angry...'

'... swearing can make things worse and can wind someone up even more...'

'... you shouldn't swear ever, but lots of people do...'

'... some people can't help it when they get angry...'

'... if you swear at someone, they might do something even worse to you...'

'... swearing doesn't solve anything, it just makes everyone angrier...'

Thinking time for children

Think about a time when you have been angry about something. What was it that made you angry? What did you do to cope with the anger? What might make you angry today? Or tomorrow? Can you do anything to stop yourself getting angry?

What made you the angriest you have ever been? Are you still angry about it? Who can you talk to if you do get angry? What does your body do when you get angry? How can you tell if someone is angry with you? What do you do about it?

Thinking time activity

Cut out a picture of a person from a magazine. Draw on their face to make them look angry. Now decide why they are angry and make up a story about what they are going to do about it.

Next, think of as many different words as you can that mean the same as 'angry'—for example, words like 'irritated' and 'aggressive'. Use a thesaurus to help you. Now put them in order, with the angriest word at the top. Can you think of times when you have felt like each of these words?

Prayer

Dear God, you gave us feelings, including anger. Help us to use anger in the right way and to get angry about the things you would get angry about.
Amen

Setting simple goals

Story summary

Jerome's gran comes to look after him while his sister is in hospital. Gran decides his bedroom needs sorting out and sets small, achievable tasks to do each evening. Through this, Jerome learns about setting goals and how good it feels when they are achieved. The story raises issues about setting achievable goals.

RE concept: Goals and motivation

 Exploring the concept

Children's understanding

- Talk about goals children have set themselves and achieved.
- Discuss what it was that motivated them to achieve their goals.

Religious overview

- Explore how people with a religious faith have specific goals related to their faith.
- Talk about what motivates people with a religious faith to achieve goals.

Christian viewpoint

Christians believe that the motivation for their faith is that Jesus conquered death so people can be friends with God for ever. A relationship with God starts here on earth, but the goal is that it continues into eternity.

Do children agree with this viewpoint?

 Key Bible verses

I have not yet reached my goal, and I am not perfect. But Christ has taken hold of me. So I keep on running and struggling to take hold of the prize. My friends, I don't feel that I have already arrived. But I forget what is behind, and I struggle for what is ahead. I run toward the goal, so that I can win the prize of being called to heaven. This is the prize that God offers because of what Christ Jesus has done.

PHILIPPIANS 3:12–14

One day, Jesus told a parable about three servants who were given money while the king went away. Two of the servants used their money wisely and were rewarded. The third servant buried his money and did nothing with it. His money was taken away from him. (Story synopsis based on Matthew 25:14–28.)

Jerome's bedroom

There were only two words to describe Jerome's bedroom. One was 'a' and the other was 'mess'. His mum and his sister moaned at him, and now his gran was moaning, too—and his gran had only arrived half an hour ago with a huge box of chocolates, a new game and a football shirt, all for him. She had come to stay for a week because his sister was having an operation and Mum needed to be free to go to visit her in hospital.

'Leave that boy to me,' Jerome heard his gran say to Mum. Jerome wasn't sure if he liked the sound of that!

The next morning, Mum took Beth to hospital and Gran took Jerome to school. 'Tonight,' Gran said as they walked down the road, 'you and I are going to start tidying your bedroom.'

That sounded so boring! Jerome hoped he was going to be allowed to do something else, too. He had a good day at school. The hamster escaped at lunchtime and he was the one who found it—inside the multi-link drawer. He told Gran about it when she picked him up. Gran grinned and told him Beth's operation had gone well and that Beth was still half asleep, which was why they weren't going to visit her that evening.

'Instead, we're going to start on your bedroom,' Gran smiled, 'and I've made a card to help us. I'll show you when we get home.'

Jerome frowned. How on earth could a card help them tidy his room?

'Monday is bookcase day,' Jerome read out loud from the card as Gran poured him a glass of milk.

'And that's all we're going to do,' Gran said. 'Just the bookcase.'

Jerome looked at Gran. Whenever Mum tidied his room, it took ages and ages and she became crosser and crosser about having to do it. Just doing the bookcase didn't sound too bad.

When they emptied the bookcase, Jerome found his favourite book about dinosaurs. He thought he had lost it or that Beth had hidden it to annoy him. He placed it next to his books about Manchester United, which were now at one end of the shelf next to his bed. On the floor was a pile of books that Jerome would never read again.

'I wonder if the children at the hospital would like to have these,' Gran said. 'Your mum could take them in tomorrow.' Jerome thought that was a good idea.

On Tuesday, Gran gave Jerome another card. It read, 'Tuesday is toybox day.'

'Let's see what we find today,' Gran laughed, as she made sure the bookcase was still tidy.

Jerome never put anything back in its box, so his plastic spacemen and his wooden train set and his mega-monsters and his soldiers were all mixed up with board games and dice and counters and bits of fluff and dead spiders and buttons and Lego and crayons and five dirty socks that were hard and smelly, and... it was a total mess.

Gran cleared a space on the carpet, heaved the box into the space and pushed it over so that everything tipped out. Then she and Jerome began sorting.

'There,' Gran said at last, 'all done.'

The toys Jerome played with most were now on the spare shelf of the bookcase. On the carpet was a pile of toys that Jerome wouldn't play with again because he had grown out of them, and in the box were things he sometimes used. The five smelly socks were in the washing basket in the bathroom. Jerome had taken them there himself.

'Shall we take these to the hospital, too?' Gran suggested, pointing at the pile of toys on the carpet. 'Your mum said we could go for evening visiting tonight.'

So they packed the toys in plastic bags and took them to the hospital. The nurses were very pleased. Beth had to lie very still, although she could talk and move her arms. She and Jerome played cards while Gran and Mum went to the canteen to find something for Mum to eat.

On Wednesday, Gran wanted to tidy and clean the carpet and everything that touched it. She pulled Jerome's bed out and vacuumed up all the fluff and dust. Then he had to help while she moved his table and rug and the boxes that lived under the windowsill. She even cleaned under and behind the cupboard where his clothes were kept.

'What are these?' she said, holding up a very muddy pair of football boots.

'My boots!' Jerome shouted. He had lost them ages ago. Mum had been so cross with him.

'Well, they were under your cupboard all the time,' Gran sighed. 'What are we going to do with you? Do they still fit?'

Jerome tried them on. They were too small now.

'My feet keep growing,' he said.

'It's what happens,' Gran commented. 'Put the boots at the top of the stairs, then come and help me put the rug back in its proper place.' He did as she asked. The room smelt fresher and cleaner.

'We can play on the floor now,' Gran said. 'Shall we make a

town? You've got some train track and a plastic road and we could make some houses out of Lego.'

Jerome showed the town to Mum when she came home later that evening. 'That's fantastic,' she said. 'Shall we leave it up for a few days? You can show Beth when she comes out of hospital on Friday.'

'Jerome,' Gran suddenly said, staring at the bookcase, 'why is there a dirty sock on your bookcase?'

They all looked. One black sock with green stripes round the top stared back at them.

'It must have jumped up there all by itself,' Jerome said.

'And where should a dirty sock be?' Gran asked.

'In the washing basket,' Jerome replied.

'So what are you going to do now?'

Jerome stood up.

'Thank you,' Gran said and smiled at Mum.

'You know what?' Gran said on Thursday as she picked Jerome up from school. 'We're going to sort through that big box of dressing-up clothes tonight.'

Gran told stories as she sorted out the clothes and Jerome dressed up as she told them. The pirate with a crooked nose fell down a hole when he was searching for treasure, the policeman caught a robber by tripping him up, and the pop star fell off the stage in the middle of his song. Gran was great at telling stories and, before they knew it, the box was tidy and put away again.

At school on Friday, Jerome was awarded a certificate because he had done so well with his maths. He grinned from ear to ear as his teacher told everyone in the class how hard he had worked.

That wasn't the only good thing to happen that day, because Gran took him shopping when he came out of school.

'What are we going to buy?' Jerome asked.

'Well, young man,' Gran smiled, 'I think you've been so

good about tidying your room, and coping with your sister being in hospital and your mum being out so much, that I want to buy you some new curtains, a new lampshade, a new notice board and a new pair of football boots. And I thought we could buy Beth a new CD. She's been very good, too.'

Today was definitely a good day!

On Saturday, Manchester United scored four goals and won their match. Jerome told Gran about it when he phoned her in the evening.

Things children have said

'... my dad told me that if you do all the big ones first, it looks like you've done more...'

'... goals help me, but I had to learn to set good ones... I mean, small ones I can achieve...'

'... to achieve makes you feel great, cheerful, on top of the world, proud. And then I want to set more goals and get there...'

'... my mum's not like his gran. My mum stands there and shouts at me. I hate tidying up, it's so boring...'

'... his gran has to help him tidy it, but not do it all. He's got to learn how to do it himself. I would do the hoovering if it were me...'

'... looking after pets goes on and on, and they always make the place untidy, and they've never heard of goals. They're dead lucky...'

'... if you achieve, you should be able to tell someone, like your mum or your dad or your best friend. Even a teacher would do...'

'... smaller goals make it quicker...'

'... you have to give yourself something that is a challenge...'

Thinking time for children

Do different people have different goals? Why? Think of a lesson you really like. What goal could you set yourself in that lesson? Think of the lesson you like least. What goal could you set for that one? Is setting goals a good idea? Why? What sort of reward would you like to give yourself for achieving your goal?

Thinking time activity

Think of some small goals to help you do something you would like to achieve. Write four goals on separate pieces of paper and pin them to a notice board, or use a fridge magnet to keep them on the fridge door until you have completed the task.

Prayer

Dear God, it's great when I manage to do something really well. I feel good inside and everyone smiles at me. It makes me want to do even more and get better. Thank you for all the things I can do. Amen

Decision making

Story summary

Lucy lives on a Greek island with her parents. They own an olive orchard and run a holiday business offering crazy golf and boat rides. During the holiday, Lucy's cousins, who are older than her, come to stay. They all help Dad with the crazy golf, but when the children are left on their own, there is trouble because decisions have to be made. This story raises issues about how good decisions are based on experience and wisdom as well as age.

RE concept: Decisions

 Exploring the concept

Children's understanding

- Talk about how children make decisions and what guides them.
- Talk about good and bad decisions they have made.

Religious overview

- Explore decisions that people with a religious faith have to make about lifestyle issues.
- Discuss how these differ between people of different faiths and those with no faith.

Christian viewpoint

Christians believe that God gives everyone different gifts and talents. Each person has to make his or her own decision how to use them and, if they do use them, they will grow in experience and expertise.

Do children agree with this viewpoint?

 Key Bible verse

God has also given each of us different gifts to use… If we can serve others, we should serve. If we can teach, we should teach. If we can encourage others, we should encourage them. If we can give, we should be generous. If we are leaders, we should do our best. If we are good to others, we should do it cheerfully.

ROMANS 12:6–8

Bible story link

The Bible records that Jesus chose twelve men to be his closest friends. They came from all walks of life. Each person came with his own unique way of following Jesus, according to the gifts that God had given him. (Story synopsis based on Matthew 4:18–22; 8:9–13 and 10:1–4.)

Stop bossing me around

Lucy was four when she left England and went to live on a Greek island. In winter her father looked after his 700 olive trees. Lucy liked it best when they harvested the crop in October. For that they worked in teams of four, stripping the olives off the trees before pruning them. Now she was eight, she was allowed to help. Some of the trees were 2000 years old. You could tell the really old ones because they had hollow insides.

The olives were collected into barrels and sold at the end of each spring, just as Lucy's father started doing his other job—running boat trips for tourists. He took holidaymakers to the south of the island looking for turtles, and on the way back they would visit the caves where minerals from the rocks made the water appear to be a deep shade of blue. He also had a crazy golf course by the beach.

Dad liked Lucy to help him with the crazy golf. She helped to collect the money and hand out putters, golf balls, score sheets and little pencils. She also helped to sweep the Astroturf if grit got on it. Their crazy golf was the best on the island, especially with the new waterfall putt that Dad had built last year. They made a good team. He was in charge and she was his helper.

That summer, Lucy's two cousins came to stay for a week. George was 13 and Sophie was 10.

'They'll probably enjoy helping us,' Dad said the day before they arrived.

They did. In fact, they loved it, polishing the boat in the morning and going on the crazy golf if no one was around. In the afternoons they went swimming in the sea and ate at the restaurant opposite the crazy golf course. Dad knew the owner, who gave them free pizzas if they helped tidy up.

Everything was going really well until Wednesday, when the olive trees needed spraying.

'Mum's going to the orchard to do the spraying and I'm doing the boat trips, which means you three are going to be in charge of the crazy golf,' Dad said as they ate their breakfast. 'George is the oldest, so he'll be in charge. Is that all right?'

Although she nodded, Lucy felt a bit hurt. She knew what to do better than George, and she spoke Greek, which he didn't. But Dad had put him in charge and that was that.

Poor Lucy. Before long, George, and then Sophie, began bossing her around.

'You sweep the course,' Sophie told her, sitting on the chair behind the kiosk.

'And when you've finished that,' George added, 'the water on the fountain hole needs topping up.' He had put himself in charge of the money and told Lucy he didn't need her in the kiosk.

'Hey, stop bossing me around,' Lucy shouted, pouting her lips. Tears were pricking the backs of her eyes.

At lunchtime, Dad came to check they were all right. His next boat trip was not until half past two.

'Everything OK?' he asked.

'Great,' George piped up. 'It's brill doing this.'

'Can one of you take your food wrappers to the bin, please, to keep the place neat and tidy?' he asked.

'I will,' Lucy said. She didn't mind doing things for her dad. Dad came with her.

'You OK?' he asked. 'You look really fed up.'

'I hate them,' she exploded. 'They boss me around all the time and ignore me if I say anything.'

Dad was a bit taken aback. 'I thought you got on all right with them.'

'It was all right until today. Today they think they're in charge, and I hate them.'

'Right,' Dad said when they returned to the kiosk and two more customers had been served. 'Here's what can happen this afternoon. Mum's still spraying the trees, but I have three spaces left in my boat. If you want, we can close the crazy golf down for a couple of hours and you can all come for a boat ride, but you'll all have to agree. I can't leave one of you here on your own. Lucy, you're too young to be left on your own, and George and Sophie don't speak Greek.'

'I vote we go on the boat,' George said straight away, loudly.

'And me,' Sophie joined in.

'And Lucy?' Dad asked.

'I want to stay here.'

Dad sighed. 'Looks like it's the boat trip,' he said. He ruffled Lucy's hair. 'I want the best for all of you, so I think you'll have to come with me.'

Lucy looked at the ground.

'Tell you what,' Dad said. 'Do you want to sit in the driver's seat with me?'

Maybe Lucy's afternoon wouldn't be so bad after all.

Things children have said

'... Dad didn't spoil Lucy. If he had, he would have let her stay, and that wasn't what the other two wanted...'

'... you want to get as many people to enjoy themselves as possible, but you have to think about what will happen tomorrow as well and if that is the right thing to do...'

'... being responsible is very important, especially if you're in charge of something and you have to think about other people. That's what my mum says...'

'... often younger people do a job better. It's practice and experience that counts...'

'... it should always be the best person...'

'... if you ask someone nicely they'll enjoy it more. Being bossy like my sister is awful...'

'... my sister has to be bossed around to make her do anything...'

'... she trusted and loved her dad...'

'... he asked her nicely and didn't boss her around like the others did...'

Thinking time for children

Who makes the decisions at school, or at home, or at a club you go to? Do you always agree with those decisions? What do you have to do if you are making a decision?

Thinking time activity

How can you best let someone know you don't agree with something they have said or a decision they have made? In pairs, role-play your ideas.

Prayer

Dear God, thank you that you have given us the ability to think and make decisions. Help us to try to do what is best for most people. More importantly, help us to be honest and treat other people as we would want to be treated ourselves. Amen

Peer group pressure

Story summary

Mitch is always getting into trouble, so when his big sister is left to babysit and invites friends round to do 'grown-up' things, he thinks he will join in. He soon realizes he is out of his depth and wishes he had stayed upstairs. The story looks at saying 'no' when those around are doing something you are uncomfortable with.

RE concept: Saying no

 ## Exploring the concept

Children's understanding

- Talk about what children think is the right behaviour in various situations.
- Explore ways of saying 'no', especially when friends apply pressure to do something children are unhappy about.
- Discuss how children's identities are formed partly by their behaviour.

Religious overview

- Explore lifestyle choices of people with religious faith, such as food restrictions or making time for religious activities.

Christian viewpoint

Christians believe that they should be careful not to get involved in worldly things that are not honouring to God.

Do children agree with this viewpoint?

 ## Key Bible verse

Don't be like the people of this world, but let God change the way you think. Then you will know how to do everything that is good and pleasing to him.

ROMANS 12:2

 ## Bible story link

In the Bible there is a story about a young man called Daniel, who was captured from Jerusalem and taken to Babylon. He soon proved to be a hard worker and rose to be an important official in the king's palace. The king's officials were jealous of

Daniel and devised a plan to have him removed. They asked King Darius to give an order that no one should worship any god except the king. Anyone not obeying this order was to be thrown to the lions.

Daniel had always prayed three times a day at his window, facing Jerusalem. He had a choice to make and decided to continue to pray as before. Before long, he was taken to the lions' pit and thrown in. King Darius then spent a sleepless night, hurrying to the pit first thing in the morning to find Daniel still alive and unharmed. (Story synopsis based on Daniel 6:1–28.)

Saying 'No!'

Mitch (or Mitchell, as he was called by his grandmother) and Marnie (or Mark, as he was called by his grandfather) were identical twins. Their feet, their hair, their elbows and their freckles were completely the same. They even had the same dimples on their knees. But inside they were as different as a staple gun is from a snail's stomach.

According to most adults, Marnie was perfect. He worked hard at school, tidied his side of the bedroom, never said anything rude and smiled at everyone he met.

'What a lovely boy your Marnie is,' people would say to Mrs Greenway, and she would smile and think how lucky she was to have him and what a brilliant mother she must be.

She needed to think that sometimes, because Mitch was exactly the opposite. He would 'break wind', as his mother called it (he and his friends called it something else), whenever he was bored, and belch in the middle of lessons. That was when he wasn't whistling quietly to himself or kicking the chair with his scuffed and muddy shoes.

Worst of all, he picked his nose and flicked whatever he found inside at people he didn't like. He was also fed up with being told he should behave like his brother.

'Why can't you be like Marnie?' people would say to him. 'Because I don't want to be,' he would think to himself. 'I want to be me. I do not want to be like my brother. I never have done and never will. So back off.'

Now Marnie and Mitch had an older sister called Jen (or Jennifer, as Mr Greenway called her when he was telling her off). Jen was 15, but she got on all right with her twin brothers even though she was six years older.

Mum and Dad sometimes left Jen to babysit because she was so sensible, and they knew she would prevent Mitch from setting the house on fire or shaving the cat or sawing the furniture in two or anything stupid like that. That Saturday evening, Jen was babysitting the twins while Mum and Dad went to the cinema.

'We'll be back about eleven,' Mum said as she and Dad put on their coats, 'and I'll phone you as soon as the film has finished to make sure everything is all right.'

'OK,' Jen called out from the living room, thinking of the ten pounds she was going to be paid. The boys had a DVD to watch and some food to eat. Then they were going to bed, and she had no intention of even thinking about them.

'Right, they've gone,' Jen shouted as the car pulled away. 'Let's get the party started!' Mitch's ears pricked up. Suddenly the DVD they were going to watch seemed very boring.

'They've gone,' his sister was saying into her mobile phone. 'Bring some drink round with you. Can you make sure everyone knows they'll have to smoke outside? I don't want Mum and Dad finding out.'

'You're not supposed to have any friends round when you're babysitting,' Marnie said indignantly.

'Shut up,' Jen said.

Marnie retreated to the settee. Mitch watched with interest. This evening could be entertaining.

Five of Jen's friends turned up, all with cans and bottles of drink. Mitch knew all her friends except one. He was taller than the others and had a scar running down his left cheek. He seemed to be older, too, and spoke gruffly. Mitch helped him lay the supplies of drink out on the kitchen table. It seemed a friendly sort of thing to do.

'Here, have some of this,' the boy offered Mitch, pouring something from a bottle into a mug.

'What is it?' Mitch asked.

The boy shrugged his shoulders. 'You too chicken to try?' he sneered.

'No!' Mitch said.

'Go on, then,' the boy said again.

'Oi, Jase, he's only nine.' Jen's voice was behind Mitch now. 'And I'm meant to be looking after him. That's not for you, Mitch.'

'Oh yes, it is,' Jase laughed. 'Here, Titch, show me how grown-up you are and drink it. All of it, mind. You're not just going to take a sip, then run away.'

'Upstairs, you,' Jen ordered, snatching the mug from Mitch's hand. 'This is my party, not yours.'

'I want my supper,' Mitch argued back.

'You can come down for it later,' Jen said, flicking her long fair hair over her shoulders. She looked a bit flustered and there was a nasty edge to her voice. Three of her friends were also in the kitchen now, with cigarettes in their mouths. She turned and unlocked the back door.

'Up,' Jen said again to Mitch.

'No,' Mitch answered back. He wanted to see if his sister was going to smoke. too. Mum had said that if Jen ever smoked, she would not be allowed out for a whole month and all her pocket money would stop.

'If you stay down, you've got to smoke one of these,' Jen said. 'Then you'll be in big trouble with Mum and Dad, because I'll tell them you smoked.'

'And I'll tell them about your friends,' Mitch answered back.

The older boy, the one Jen had called Jase, suddenly put his hands under Mitch's armpits, dragged him outside and held him against the outside wall of the house.

'Going to have your first cigarette, then, are you?' There was something dangerous about the way he spat the words out. 'Or are you going to tell Mummy and Daddy about your big sister having a few friends round while looking after the babies?'

A red light was glowing by Jen's face as she sucked in. Her other friends were out there too, smoking, watching, laughing at him. Mitch felt the smoke disappearing up his nose like a bogeyman with nowhere to go but inside him.

'Let me go!' Mitch suddenly shouted and began wriggling and punching the air with his fists. Jase laughed again and let him go.

'I'm telling Mum of you!' Mitch shouted at Jen.

'If you tell your mother anything, I'm going to beat your nose so it hangs off your fat little face,' Jase snarled, his fingers grabbing Mitch's shoulders as he reached the back door. 'Jen told you to get up to bed and you didn't, so...'

'Leave him, Jase,' Jen said. 'He's only teasing you, Mitch.'

She stuffed a ten-pound note into Mitch's hand. 'Get upstairs and keep this and don't say a word. Got it?'

Mitch knew where that money had come from—Mum's purse. He had seen Jen open the drawer where Mum kept her handbag earlier that evening. He ducked down, out of Jase's grasp, and threw himself through the back door.

'He won't tell Mum or Dad.' That was Jen's voice mocking him. 'We'll be all right.'

Mitch was upstairs in ten seconds—one second for every

pound he had just been given. Marnie looked up from the book he was reading.

'What's going on?' he asked.

'Nothing much,' Mitch said, trying to breathe normally.

'I'm glad I came upstairs, then,' Marnie sighed.

Mitch put the television on and started the DVD, but he didn't watch it. He didn't want to be a 'perfect' like Marnie, but at that moment he didn't trust Jen either. He had seen a different side to her tonight and, even though he was only nine and did lots of things himself that were naughty, he didn't want to do what she was doing.

Mitch didn't have any supper. He didn't dare go downstairs again. When the DVD had finished, he crept into bed and lay there wide awake. He heard Jen's friends leave and, a few minutes later, Mum and Dad's car come back.

At breakfast the next morning, Mum commented that ten pounds had disappeared from her handbag. She asked if anyone knew anything about it.

Things children have said

'... you've got to be strong to do what you really think is right. It's really hard...'

'... never, ever, ever drink something you're not happy about. If you do, it might be a drug...'

'... you shouldn't trust people you don't know...'

'... you shouldn't always trust people you do know...'

'... you have to think what will happen next...'

'... my brother was like that big boy once and tried to get me to do things I didn't want to, only I told Mum and he got it in the neck...'

'... think what you have been told by your parents...'

'... you have to think about it and make a sensible decision. But you don't always have the time to think about it, so you have to think about it before you get there...'

'... ask someone what they think, but make sure they are trustworthy and see if they think the same as you...'

'... it's very hard sometimes. Sometimes it's easy and you just know...'

'... my mum trusts me when I'm with Sarah because she says if there are two of you saying 'no' it's easier, and she trusts Sarah and knows her mum and dad...'

'... he should have given the ten-pound note back to his mum and told her everything...'

'... I would have kept quiet, but put the money back when she wasn't looking...'

Thinking time for children

What would you have done if you were Mitch? Have you ever been asked to do something you thought wasn't safe? What did you do? What should you do if you are not happy about something that is happening around you? Where is the safest place you know? Who is the safest person you know? Who might put pressure on you to do something unsafe?

Thinking time activity

Act out scenes where you have to say 'no' to something. Draw round your hand. On each of the fingers and thumb, write the name of someone you can trust.

Prayer

Dear God, it's really hard sometimes to say 'no' when everyone else is doing something and I want to join in. I want to be the same as them, even though I know it's not right. Help me be strong and brave. Amen

Personal hygiene

Story summary

Smodge is a little creature who refuses to take care of himself until the Green Blob arrives to offer advice. The story raises personal hygiene and healthy eating issues.

RE concept: Healthy lifestyle

 Exploring the concept

Children's understanding
❂ Talk about the children's favourite foods.
❂ Discuss foods that are good for children to eat.

Religious overview
❂ Talk about foods that people with a religious faith eat (and don't eat).
❂ Explore why certain foods are eaten (and not eaten) and what this signifies.
❂ Discuss how food brings communities and families together in support and celebration.

Christian viewpoint
Christians believe that the human body is like a temple to God and that people should look after their bodies. In this way, they will bring honour to God.

Do children agree with this viewpoint?

 Key Bible verses

So let's come near God with pure hearts and a confidence that comes from having faith. Let's keep our hearts pure... and our bodies washed with clean water.

HEBREWS 10:22

You know that your body is a temple where the Holy Spirit lives. The Spirit is in you and is a gift from God. You are no longer your own. God paid a great price for you. So use your body to honour God.

1 CORINTHIANS 6:19–20

Bible story link

When Daniel was taken from Jerusalem to Babylon as a slave, he was chosen to serve in the royal palace and eat the same food as those in the palace. He requested to be allowed to eat only vegetables. After ten days, his appearance was compared with those who had eaten the rich foods laid on at the palace. Daniel was far healthier and allowed to continue his vegetarian diet. (Story synopsis based on Daniel 1:1–16.)

Smodge has a wash

Once upon a time, in the land where funny things happen, there lived some little creatures. People never saw them, but they were definitely there. They were about eight centimetres tall, covered in hair and with two eyes on brightly coloured stalks coming out of their cheeks.

Smodge was one of these little creatures. One day, at the beginning of the summer holidays, Smodge climbed into one of the houses along the cobbled street and sniffed. No cat. No dog. Good. This was a safe house to live in.

Smodge hunted around until he found a cracked floorboard in the spare bedroom. Underneath it was a dirty hole, full of cobwebs and dust.

'What a lovely place to live,' he said out loud and dropped his bags into what was to become his new home. Humbo, Latso and Jimpsy already lived in the house, in the cupboard under the stairs.

'Only one human lives here,' they told him, 'and he's out most of the time, but he eats fantastic food. Come on, we'll show you how to get into the fridge.'

Smodge's eyes nearly dropped off their stalks when he saw what was waiting to be eaten. Chocolate cake, cream cheese, chocolate gateau, biscuits, chocolate mousse, mayonnaise, chocolate pudding. And that was just the bottom shelf.

'When do I start?' he asked. Jimpsy was showing him where the cereal, bread and fruit were kept, but Smodge was not interested in those.

'Smodge,' Jimpsy said, 'you must eat other things, too.'

'Stop it!' Smodge interrupted, a little rudely. 'You sound just like my mother, and she was a right bore—always telling me what I must eat. If this yummy food is here, why eat anything different?'

'Just don't eat too much, otherwise the human will know we've been here,' Latso warned. 'And then he might get a cat or something to chase us out.'

'OK,' Smodge spluttered from the top of the chocolate cake where he was stuffing crumbs into his mouth.

After a few minutes, Humbo decided it was time to move their new friend on.

'We'll show you where the leaking tap is so that you can wash yourself,' he said.

'I won't be needing that,' Smodge laughed. 'My mother made me wash every morning and every evening. Waste of water if you ask me—and she's not here to nag, so I'm not washing any more.'

The others took a step closer to the chocolate cake and breathed in—sweat, bad breath, smelly feet. It was not a happy smell.

'I really must be going,' Humbo said.

'Me too,' Jimpsy added.

'OK,' said Smodge. 'See you around.'

'Not if I can help it,' Latso whispered.

It was a shame, because the little creatures often had parties and midnight feasts. They went out for walks and organized football matches against the creatures who lived in the house across the street. Sometimes they filled the sink up with water and had diving competitions. But Smodge was never invited to join in.

'I wonder if he can swim,' Jimpsy said one day.

'No way,' Humbo laughed. 'He hates water.'

'I feel sorry for him,' Latso said. 'I haven't seen or spoken to him for ages.'

'I've seen him,' Jimpsy said. 'He's enormous and you can smell him a mile off.'

Smodge knew, deep down, that everyone was avoiding him. Before long, he stopped going out during the day. He would creep into the kitchen at night, where even the cheese held its breath when it smelt him coming. Smodge told himself he preferred the dark, but that was not the real reason, and as time passed he grew smellier, lonelier and more overweight. If it had not been for the fact that someone was watching over him, he would have stayed like that for ever.

One day there was a knock on the cracked floorboard. 'Someone's come to visit me,' Smodge thought. He waddled across to the floorboard and pushed it up. Lying on the floor was a tube of toothpaste and a bright yellow toothbrush.

'What are these for?' Smodge muttered to himself. 'My mother used to make me use them.' He started to feel cross.

'I'm not using them,' he said out loud and left the brush where it was. Then he took the lid off the toothpaste and jumped on it. A stream of paste squirted on to the floorboard like a white-and-blue snake.

The toothpaste snake lay there all night and all the following morning. It watched as someone knocked on the floorboard at a quarter to three in the afternoon. Smodge waddled to the floorboard and pushed it up again. But all he saw was a can of deodorant spray lying between the toothbrush and the toothpaste snake.

'I don't need this, either,' he shouted and used it as a rolling-pin to flatten the snake. Then he went back into his hole, where he sat very still for a long time.

Next day, very early, he pulled himself up on to the floorboards and rolled into the shadows under the spare bed. He sat there all day, watching and waiting. Nothing happened. Absolutely nothing. The sun shone all day and, soon after it had gone to bed, pale moonlight fell across the cracked floorboard.

'I'm absolutely fed up and...'

It was then that the Green Blob turned up. She sat, cross-legged, on the floor next to the rolled-out toothpaste snake. Smodge noticed the 992 sequins sewn on her dress. They looked rather pretty.

'How long have you been there?' he asked in a surprised voice.

'Ages and ages,' she whispered. Smodge was quite taken with her deep husky voice. She winked at him and flashed a dazzling smile in his direction.

'You can only see me if you're ready to listen to what I have to say,' she carried on.

'I'm listening,' Smodge breathed.

'And sweating,' Green Blob said. 'I can smell it. Fresh sweat on dried armpits is not very pleasant. Can you move back a bit, please?'

Smodge was a bit taken aback. He had heard about Green Blob. His mother had told him about her.

'You are unhappy,' she whispered. 'I've come to see if I can help. Tell me why you are sad.'

'I want a friend,' Smodge sighed. 'But no one ever talks to me or comes near me.'

'I'm not surprised,' Green Blob said. 'You stink, your breath smells, you eat all the wrong foods and you do not care about yourself. Now let me give you something.' And out of her bag she pulled a tube of toothpaste and a new toothbrush.

'I've got one of those,' Smodge said crossly.

'I know, I gave it to you two days ago.'

'Well, I'm not going to use it.'

'Well, you will carry on stinking and no one will ever come near you,' Green Blob said in a gentle tone. 'And I will disappear again.'

'Oh,' Smodge whispered.

'And if I disappear I'll never come back.'

'Oh,' Smodge whispered.

'I've brought some other things to help you look after yourself.'

'Oh,' Smodge whispered again.

'Smodge,' Green Blob asked, 'do you think you're worth looking after?'

Smodge thought for a moment.

'I don't know,' he said.

'You are, you know. Your parents looked after you when you were little. You've got to do it for yourself now.'

And with that, Green Blob vanished. She just disappeared. Smodge sighed and looked at what she had given him. He thought for a few minutes.

'OK,' he said out loud to no one in particular. 'I'm going to go to the leaking tap and I'm taking this lot with me.'

Behind the curtains, Green Blob smiled to herself.

'You do that,' she whispered in her deep husky voice.

Things children have said

'... you should wash every morning and every afternoon...'

'... people who don't look after themselves are sad inside...'

'... he should eat bread, fruit, vegetables, salad, meat, cereals...'

'... you can eat chocolate if you aren't too fat and don't have too much of it...'

'... people eat meat as long as they're not a vegetarian...'

'... Smodge knew he was dirty but wouldn't do anything about it. He was ashamed of himself and hoped no one would see him at night...'

'... he hoped no one would smell him in the dark. He was wrong because they could...'

'... he didn't like being with people any more...'

'... if you don't use it, your teeth will get rotten and fall out...'

'... clean yourself. I would say it very loudly as well...'

'... he needs shampoo as well as liquid soap and some of that smelly stuff like my brother uses...'

Thinking time for children

Think about how you look after yourself. Is there any way you could do better? Do you need help to find out how to look after yourself? Who could you ask for advice? Sometimes, washing is seen as a symbol for being clean on the inside. How does it feel when you know you are friends with everyone and feel good about who you are?

Thinking time activity

Make a list of all the things you need to look after yourself properly, including food. When and why do you need them? If you were going away, which things would you take and in which order of importance would you put them? Why? Is everyone's list the same? If not, why not?

Prayer

Dear God, you have made us, and our bodies are brilliant. Help us to look after ourselves in the best way we possibly can. Help us to be clean on the inside as well as the outside. Amen

Just teasing?

Story summary

Under the sea, everyone loves and respects Oscar the whale. His damaged flipper and glasses are never mentioned—they are just part of him. That all changes when the newest mermaid arrives and starts teasing him about his appearance. Before long, the teasing turns into bullying, until one day Oscar disappears. Eventually, the smallest fish in the shoal finds him and begs him to return. Children are left to decide whether Oscar does return and what support is given to the newest mermaid to help her stop bullying. The story looks at how teasing can become bullying and raises issues of how to deal with it.

RE concept: Relationships

 Exploring the concept

Children's understanding

- ✪ Talk about the ingredients that go to make good relationships and friendships with other people.
- ✪ Talk about what happens when this goes wrong.
- ✪ Discuss the difference between laughing with someone and laughing at them.
- ✪ In general terms, think of examples of teasing that is all right and bullying that is not.

Religious overview

- ✪ Discuss how relationships within a faith community are organized with leaders, social events and family bonds.
- ✪ Talk about the roles different people play, how those roles are respected by others and how a good leader would put an end to bullying.

Christian viewpoint

Christians believe that God wants people to love each other as much as they love themselves, which means treating other people as we would want them to treat us.

Do children agree with this viewpoint?

 Key Bible verse

Be friendly with everyone. Don't be proud and feel that you are cleverer than others. Make friends with ordinary people. Don't ill-treat someone who has ill-treated you. But try to earn the respect of others, and do your best to live at peace with everyone.

ROMANS 12:16–18

Joseph was the favoured son of Jacob. His father gave him a special long-sleeved coat, which signified that he did not have to work in the fields, despite being the next-to-youngest son. His brothers were jealous and bullied him, their final act of bullying being to sell him as a slave to some Ishmaelite merchants on their way to Egypt. (Story synopsis based on Genesis 37:1–28.)

Oscar goes missing

Once, long ago, in the water between the Mystical Island and the Island Beyond, the fishes and mermaids were called to a meeting beside the deserted castle. Something had happened—something that had never happened before and something that worried them all. Whale had disappeared.

'He'll be somewhere,' the chief mermaid said.

'But where?' whispered the mermaid with bunches in her hair.

'We'll find him,' added the mermaid with the silver wig. 'He's different from any other whale I know.'

Oscar certainly was different. For a start, he had a deep scar running down one of his flippers, and he wore glasses because he was short-sighted. Then there was his voice, which was all squeaky, and his eating habits, which were very strange. Would you believe that his favourite meal was sprouts and apricot jam on toast?

'I think we ought to look for him,' the golden cod said. 'He's been gone for over a week now.' Suddenly they all realized how much they were missing him. Whale was always friendly. He laughed with them, listened to them and helped them. Sometimes they teased him, not because they were laughing at him but because they were laughing with him.

'Hello,' the mermaids would say in a squeaky voice just like his, 'and how are you today?'

'Having a whale of a time,' Oscar would reply and give them a ride on his back.

The fish called him O-scar because of his damaged flipper. He didn't mind that because he knew they were only teasing him.

'O-scar, what funny flippers you have,' they would say.

'All the better to flip you with,' he would laugh and flip them through the water. It was like having their very own theme park ride in the depths of the sea, and Oscar was happy because he knew he was loved and that everyone cared about him.

But now Oscar had disappeared. No one thought anything of it at first. He sometimes went off to see his friends on the other side of the islands, but it was strange for him not to have told anyone where he had gone.

The newest mermaid combed her hair. She had joined them only two weeks ago. Oscar had helped her find somewhere to put the seven suitcases and three big boxes she had brought with her when she first arrived.

'You're very quiet,' the mermaid with the silver wig suddenly said to her.

The newest mermaid carried on combing her hair.

'I said, you're very quiet,' the mermaid with the silver wig tried again.

'I think I upset him,' the newest mermaid said, looking at the sand beneath her tail.

Everyone turned to look at her. No one ever upset Oscar.

'What did you say?' asked the mermaid with bunches in her hair.

'I told him his scar made him look stupid.'

'You told him what?'

'Well it does, doesn't it? It makes him look all funny. And he was annoying me because I wanted some apricot jam and I thought he might take it all. You know how much he eats.'

'There are always pots of jam in the food store,' the chief mermaid breathed, and the anger on her face shimmered through the water. 'That scar will never be stupid,' she added under her breath. 'Do you know how he got it?'

The newest mermaid shook her head.

'Three of us got trapped in the fishermen's nets and he rescued us. That's how he hurt himself. He got caught when he was helping us.'

There was silence. The mermaids and the fish looked at each other, then looked at the newest mermaid.

'You have said something to make Oscar feel small,' the chief mermaid said. 'You have hurt him and you did it deliberately. Therefore you are a bully.'

The other mermaids gasped. Being called a bully, especially by the chief mermaid, was unheard of. They all knew that bullies were sad inside, so sad that they had to be nasty to others to try to make themselves feel better.

'What are we going to do about Oscar?' the golden cod asked. They would deal with the newest mermaid later on. Oscar was far more important than this bully who had come to live with them.

'We're going to search for him,' the chief mermaid said. 'And when we find him, we'll tell him how incredibly special he is.'

And that is what they did. They swam behind the great mountain where the sprout and carrot fields basked in the golden sun. They dived beneath the great rocks where treasure lay in wooden cases. They wriggled inside the jagged caves where the shipwreck was. The golden cod even went to the far side of the furthest island, but Oscar was nowhere to be found.

Eventually, it was the smallest fish in the shoal who found him. Oscar was lying by one of the goals on the football pitch, his eyes closed and his tail quivering. He was crying.

'Please come back,' the smallest fish whispered. 'We need you. That newest mermaid told us what she said to you. She's a bully and there is no way she will be allowed to say anything like that to you again. Please come back.'

Things children have said

'... bullying is calling people names in a sarcastic voice and threatening them...'

'... bullies are sad inside. I stick with my friends and then no one bullies me...'

'... if your best mate comes round and he's got a new football scarf and you say "that's horrible", but he knows you well enough to ignore you and that you're being honest... but you have to know each other well enough to be able to do that...'

'... I think Oscar should go back and the newest mermaid should apologize to him in front of everyone...'

'... he would come back because he missed all his friends...'

'... I think she said sorry to Oscar and everyone was friends again. The newest mermaid didn't know what she was doing. She should have a second chance and prove she isn't nasty...'

'... teasing isn't nasty and it's fun, but bullying hurts people...'

'... I think she left where she was living because she didn't have any friends, because no one had ever taught her how to make friends and what you have to do to get them. You have to think about other people to get friends...'

'... I don't know why, but I think she became Oscar's closest friend...'

'... some bullies aren't bullies all the time, just for a bit...'

'... you should tell someone if you are being bullied. I told my teacher and my mum when I was bullied in Year 2...'

Thinking time for children

What do you think Oscar did next, and why? What could the others do to stop the newest mermaid bullying Oscar? What would you have said to the newest mermaid? What would you have said to Oscar? When does teasing become bullying? When have you been teased? Did you like being teased?

Thinking time activity

Use puppets to act out a situation where teasing becomes bullying.

Prayer

Dear God, help me to know the difference between teasing and bullying and to be kind to other people. Amen

Bullying

Story summary

Spid is a special spider with multicoloured legs. When she arrives in the wood, she is given four pairs of matching wellies. However, setting off to explore the wood is not the happy experience she expects. To her horror, she soon realizes that everyone in the wood bullies everyone else. Each time she cries, her tears wash away the pattern on the wellies until they become hard and impossible to remove. At that point Spid, too, begins to bully others. The owner of the wood rescues her when the wood catches fire. First of all, he removes her wellies. Then he shows her the path to freedom. The story confronts reasons for bullying and suggests that everyone can start again and move on.

RE concept: Freedom

 ## Exploring the concept

Children's understanding
- Talk about how children define the word 'freedom'.
- Discuss what restricts the children's freedom and why.
- Talk about who spoils their freedom and lead the discussion into bullying.

Religious overview
- Explore how faith communities view freedom and what people with a religious faith strive to be released from.

Christian viewpoint
Christians believe that God wants them to be the best that they can be. To live life to the full, people need to be free from fear and oppression from others.

Do children agree with this viewpoint?

 ## Key Bible verse

'You will know the truth, and the truth will set you free.'
JOHN 8:32

 ## Bible story link

At the end of the story of Joseph, his brothers, who bullied him when he was younger and sold him to be a slave in Egypt, came to Egypt to buy corn when there was a famine. They didn't recognize Joseph but eventually he told them who he was. Their father had been told (by the brothers) that Joseph was dead. Jacob was an elderly man when his sons finally told the truth. When he discovered that Joseph was alive and living in Egypt, he was released from the secret his sons had held from him. Only then was he free to move on from the consequences of their bullying. (Story synopsis based on Genesis 37—46.)

The wellies

Spid was a beautiful spider. She had fine, silky fur all over her body and long, strong legs. It was a Monday when she arrived in the wood.

The first things she noticed were the brightly coloured wellies. They were not making any noise or anything like that. They were just there, next to her—all eight of them. As it was not raining, she decided they could stay where they were. She could always come back for them later if need be.

The grass tickled her furry little legs as she scuttled through the undergrowth. She liked the feel of it as she went up over little stones, under soft green leaves, round tiny clumps of toadstools, until she came to a clearing where she stopped to draw breath. She felt alive, happy and free as she arched her back so that the warm sun could rest on it. 'All I need now is a friend,' she thought.

At that moment there was a rustling in the grass behind her.

'Hello,' Spid said, turning to see who it was. 'I've just arrived here and my name's Spid. Would you like to be my frie…?'

She stopped as an enormous shadow blocked out the sun and a pair of black wellies ground to a halt in front of her. They belonged to a rather large beetle.

'I don't need anyone, let alone a friend,' it spat at her.

'Why not?' Spid asked.

'Because friends always let you down.'

'I wouldn't,' Spid said. She could not imagine what life must be like without friends.

'You would,' the beetle said, swinging its front wellie at Spid's face. 'You'd be like everyone else. Now get out of my way, you stupid, pathetic, pea-brained, scumbag little spider.' Then it disappeared into the long grass.

Spid stayed where she was for a few minutes, clutching her throbbing face until the pain began to ease off. There was a noise like someone sniffing. She looked up to see who it was.

A big spider was leaning against a stone at the edge of the clearing, watching her. He, too, wore wellies—black muddy ones, like the beetle's.

'If you've just arrived in this wood, you've got a lot to learn, haven't you?' he said.

'Have I?' Spid said.

'Why haven't you got your wellies on, for a start?' he asked her.

'Because it isn't raining,' Spid whispered back.

'Oh dear,' he sneered. 'You're very small, aren't you, and a bit stupid. Spid the kid with a face like a dustbin lid. Huh! In this wood, wellies aren't for keeping the rain out.'

'What are they for, then?'

The big spider shrugged.

'To stop you being hurt some of the time and to kick out at others the rest. Like that beetle did to you just then. Makes you feel big when you lash out, especially when you find someone who's scared of you. But I'll tell you something, seeing as you're new around here. If you're going to smash someone up, make sure they're not going to tell someone else about it. Because if they do go telling, you could get into big— and I mean big—trouble yourself. Have you got that?

'So where are your wellies?' the big spider asked again.

'Back there,' Spid said, pointing in the direction she had come from.

'And I suppose they're all bright colours?' he asked, and started laughing when Spid nodded. It was a bitter, nasty laugh.

'All wellies are like that to start with. They'll soon go black like everyone else's. You'll see.'

Spid suddenly remembered something. 'Would you be my friend?' she asked him.

The big spider said nothing for a minute. Then he lowered his head and walked towards her. Spid waited, wondering what he was going to do.

'Push off,' he spat when he reached her. 'In this wood, no one has friends.'

For a brief moment, Spid stared into the hard, sad expression on the spider's face. It made her shiver. She turned and ran, back to where her own pairs of wellies were. No miserable old black ones for her. She had something far better—she was not going to let them go black.

The pair with red and yellow stripes went on her front legs; the ones with green and gold spots were second, followed by the ones with silver and turquoise circles. The blue and pink diamonds went at the back. They looked fantastic. Maybe wearing wellies would not be so bad after all.

Spid thought about the beetle and the spider and how nasty they had been to her. 'Is everyone in this beautiful wood like them?' she wondered. She hoped not, yet she did not want anyone else being horrible to her. So what could she do?

In the end, she decided to hide if anyone came near her, just in case. She would leave finding a friend until later.

With that thought, she set off once more. The wellies got in the way a bit and she could not run freely as she had before, but they were quite soft and comfortable and she definitely felt safer in them. Besides, they would be very useful if it came on to rain.

Spid enjoyed her day. There were so many new and exciting things to find out about that she forgot how awful the beetle and big spider had been. However, one thing puzzled her and that was the huge wall. Whichever direction she travelled in, she always came to it. She tried to climb over it at first, but it was covered with something so slippery that she always ended up sliding back down again and never reached the top.

'Is this wall here to keep everyone in, or to keep something out?' she wondered. By the time evening came, Spid was very tired. She found a nice leaf to curl up under and settled down. She breathed in deeply, closed her eyes and drifted off to sleep.

'I'll rip your legs off one by one if you don't move,' a voice snarled at her. Startled, Spid opened her eyes as a shudder of fear ran through her. A snail, his whole body covered in one thick, black wellie, towered above, staring down at her.

'Look at you,' it sneered. 'You're so frightened.'

Spid did not wait to hear more. Trembling all over, she started to run. She ran and ran and ran, as fast as her wellied legs would carry her. She did not care where she went and did not see the hole waiting for her. She twisted on to her back as she fell. Down, down she went until she lay in a pile of dust at the bottom.

'Why is everyone nasty to me?' she sobbed. 'All I want is a friend. Someone I can trust and who likes me because I'm me.'

Her tears trickled down her face, and as each one fell it rolled on to her wellies as though washing them. Soon the shine came off, and then the colours began to fade and before long the red and yellow stripes, green and gold spots, silver and turquoise circles and pink and blue diamonds had completely disappeared, washed away by her tears.

In the darkness, Spid carried on crying until there were no tears left. Then she fell asleep. Night passed and dawn brought a new day with it. Spid woke up and crawled out of the hole.

'Right,' she said, 'this is a new day and I'm going...'

Then she stopped, staring at her wellies. They were hard and uncomfortable. She tried to shake them off but they wouldn't move. They were completely stuck to her legs and, worst of all, they had become... black. The more Spid stared at her wellies, the angrier she became. All thoughts of trying to find a friend or exploring the wood were gone. Someone had taken her beautiful, soft wellies away and left these horrible black ones instead.

It was at that moment that the unfortunate little caterpillar appeared. He was vivid pink, with gorgeous long black hair that stuck up, and his feet were covered with loads of pairs of brightly coloured wellies. Each one was a different colour and he loved them. He had been trying to eat a dead leaf and had just decided that soft green ones tasted better than the brown crunchy ones.

'Hello,' he said to Spid in a chirpy voice. 'I've just arrived here and I'm finding out about the wood. Do you want to come and join me?'

Spid stared at him. How dare this little caterpillar speak to her like that? How dare he be happy when she was not? How dare he wear those wellies that were so bright, when hers were black?

She lowered her head and spat at him, nearly blowing him over. Then she laughed out loud and made fun of his pink-and-black body, watching with delight as his face crumpled and he started to cry. One of his tears rolled down the outside of his front right wellie, and the gold and red spots now had a black line through them where the colours had been washed away.

'Isn't it wonderful?' Spid thought. 'He's scared of me. He's little and I'm big and I'm in control. I am so powerful and clever.' She kicked him as hard as she could. He cried out in pain, so she lashed out again, just for fun, then told him to get lost.

Spid was part of the wood now. She was showing everyone she could survive and nobody need ever know how much she was hurting, deep inside, and how she had once wanted a friend. Finding a nice patch of soft moss under an overgrown bush, she made it her own. It was by the big oak tree to the left-hand side of the path and she was rarely disturbed. Spid was happy to spend the rest of her days there, living on her own.

But that was not to be, for other things had been planned. It was a Saturday when it happened.

The day started just like any other day. The sun rose, the dew on the grass glistened and Spid poked her nose out from under the bush. But there was something in the air that morning. She sniffed. What was it? A strange crackling noise filled her ears.

Suddenly she knew. Fire! Spid scuttled on to the path and gasped as a wall of hazy heat greeted her. She had to get away—fast.

She raced along the path as quickly as she could, her heart pounding and straining as she tried to go faster, faster, but her wellies kept getting in the way. They were too heavy, too cumbersome. She could hardly spin a web in them, let alone escape from flames that were flickering not far behind her.

Eventually she had to stop and it was as she lay gasping for breath that she remembered the wall. There was no way of getting over it, was there?

'What am I going to do?' she whispered. 'No one will miss me anyway, so what does it matter?'

'I'd miss you,' a voice said.

Spid looked up. A person was sitting with his back against a broken tree stump just in front of her.

'I'd miss you,' he calmly said again, looking straight back at her.

'Who are you?' Spid said, crossly.

She wondered what on earth he was doing, sitting with his back against a tree stump that was about to be destroyed by scorching flames. Didn't he know there was a fire? Couldn't he feel the heat and hear the roaring noise it was making?

'So, who are you?' she demanded again.

'I'm the owner of the wood,' he replied, rather sadly. Spid had to listen really carefully to catch what he said.

'You're the owner,' she repeated, just to make sure she had heard him correctly. The man nodded. If he was the owner, she thought, maybe he could help her.

'How do I get out, then?' she shouted. 'How do I get over that wall you've put all the way round it?'

He sighed.

'I didn't build that wall,' he said. 'This wood used to be such a beautiful place. Then things changed. All the creatures that live here decided to wear wellies and to build the wall. I made a hole in it a while back so you could escape, but not many of you found it.'

'Bet I can find it!' Spid shouted up at him. Maybe there was a way to escape after all.

'How will you find it?' he asked as she drew level with his feet.

Spid stopped and they stared at each other while she tried to think of an answer.

'I don't know,' she finally whispered.

'I could tell you where it is if you wanted me to,' he said, 'but I'm not shouting above the roar of these flames. You'll have to let me pick you up so we can talk properly.'

Spid was not sure she wanted to be picked up just then. She really wanted to be on her way. Yet she had to find out where the hole was, otherwise she would be burnt alive.

The man was lowering his hand for her to climb on to so that he could pick her up. She gasped when she saw his hand. The skin was lumpy and scarred and it looked as if something had been pushed right through the bones. He seemed to know what she was thinking.

'I was wounded while I was making the hole in the wall,' he said. 'It's all right, it doesn't hurt any more.'

'Oh,' she said.

'You've got to take your wellies off,' he said once she was level with his nose. 'Then you can run faster.'

'But you have to wear wellies in this wood,' Spid said.

'I don't wear any,' he replied.

Spid peered over the side of his hand. He was right. He did not wear wellies, and his feet were damaged, too, like his hands. They were going to get damaged again if he didn't hurry up. They would be burnt. So would hers, for the fire was now only about twelve trees away and sparks were floating in the air.

'We're running out of time,' the owner said softly.

'Yes,' Spid thought. 'We are.' Why was he wasting time by telling her to take her wellies off when she knew she couldn't because they were stuck to her legs? Why didn't he just tell her where the hole in the wall was?

'My wellies are sort of part of me,' Spid said. 'They won't come off.'

Suddenly she was filled with a longing to escape. She wanted to get away, to start again—to be free. She wanted to have friends she could trust, friends who did not wear black wellies. Suddenly she said, 'Can you pull the wellies off for me?'

The owner smiled at her. Spid found herself smiling back. It was the first time she had ever smiled a real smile, but it faded quickly as he began to tug at one of her front wellies. It hurt. It hurt a lot. Spid screamed out in pain as he pulled.

'You're hurting me,' she cried.

'I know, but I have to get you out of these wellies,' he said gently.

'What colour were they before they went black?' he asked.

'I've forgotten,' she whispered. 'I know I liked them, though. They were really pretty.'

'Those ones were red with yellow stripes,' he said and chuckled to himself. The last time Spid had seen her front legs, they had been soft, furry and a dull sort of brown colour. Now they were still soft, they were still furry, but they had become the most exquisite shade of red with bright yellow stripes going from top to bottom.

'Let's see what else those wellies are covering up,' he said and began pulling the others off, one by one.

'My beautiful little friend,' he whispered as the last one was removed.

Spid looked down at the array of turquoise and silver and red and yellow and green and gold and pink and blue beneath her. She was beautiful, and she trembled with pleasure as she stood there in the palm of his hand.

Gently he lowered her to the ground. The grass tickled her legs as it had when she'd first arrived in the wood. It felt even lovelier now.

'See that path,' he showed her. 'You'll come to the hole in the wall if you go down there.'

Spid looked in amazement. She had never seen the path before.

'Thank you,' she shouted at the top of her voice. She had to shout to be heard above the noise of the fire. It was so close now, but she was not worried. At last her legs were free and she was able to run and jump and be free. Most of all, she could escape.

'Where are you going?' she asked him.

'Around,' he said, and smiled at her again. 'Just around. Now off you go.'

Spid did not need telling twice. As she disappeared down the path, the owner stood up. He took the black wellies in his hands and threw them deep, deep into the fire. Spid's were not the only ones he had taken off that day. Neither would they be the last.

Like the others, the wellies melted and bubbled and sizzled until they were no more.

Things children have said

'... bullies are sad people because they are being bullied as well and that's why they have to bully us...'

'... people have black wellies so they can hide better...'

'... bullies always wear black wellies...'

'... my wellies would be different blues with yellow spots, lavender and yellow, white with little gold stars on, elephant shapes with white circles all round them, yellow with blue bobbles that light up. Or I might have zigzags, pink with beautiful teddy bears all over them, all sorts and a different pair every single day...'

'... I'd never ever want to have black ones on because they're the sort that bullies wear...'

'... he had a friend once, but the friend let him down and now he doesn't need them. But he does really...'

'... it's not nice when someone's nasty to you. My big brother's like that and Mum has to tell him off. She says he's got to grow up...'

'... I was scared of someone down our road. Then my mum went to see his mum and now he leaves me alone...'

'... kicking out and being horrible is what bullies do...'

'... bullies pick on other people because they haven't got any friends. If you stick with your friends, they're less likely to say nasty things...'

'... if someone's horrible to you, you have got to tell someone straight away. It's no good waiting or it gets worse. I'd tell my mum or my teacher. The head teacher's even better. Head teachers are fierce. My mum says they eat little children who don't behave as they should, only they wouldn't eat me, just someone who bullied me...'

'... the bullies made Spid feel small and sad and then he hurt her...'

'... she was nice underneath and everyone around her was horrible and she doesn't really want to be horrible because she's not like that really...'

'... Spid's wellies stop other animals hurting her and make her feel big so she can smash up other little animals like the ones that are smaller than her...'

Thinking time for children

Think about what you would like to be free from. Is there anything you know you really ought to tell someone about? Think about who you could tell.

Thinking time activity

Draw a pair of wellies. On one, write down how you can help a bully stop bullying. Imagine that this is like taking his or her wellies off. On the other, write down what you would do if you were bullied. Imagine how it would feel if your beautiful wellies were turning black.

Prayer

Dear God, if I am sad about something, please help me to tell someone. Thank you that I can always tell you about anything and you will still love me. If someone keeps being nasty to me, help me to stand up for myself and to try to be nice to them at the same time, even though that's very difficult. Amen

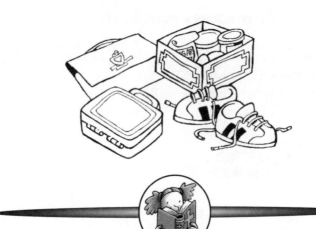

Stranger danger

Story summary

Anjali has a lot of things to carry to school and is offered a lift by someone she has seen her mother talking to. She accepts. The narrative leaves Anjali in the back of the car and raises issues about stranger danger.

RE concept: Evil

 ## Exploring the concept

Children's understanding

- ✪ Talk about what children think the word 'evil' means.
- ✪ Discuss evil things that happen in the world. Put them into a list, with the most evil at the top.
- ✪ Talk about what to do if children find themselves in a dangerous situation and whether it is always easy to do the right thing.

Religious overview

- ✪ Explore how faith communities perceive evil and how it affects the world we live in.

Christian viewpoint

Christians believe that people live in a constant spiritual battle between good and evil. God represents everything that is good, holy and pure. The devil represents everything that is evil and destructive. Through his life, death and resurrection, Jesus has put the power of the devil under God's control, but people still need to be on their guard against evil.

Do children agree with this viewpoint?

 ## Key Bible verses

Let the mighty strength of the Lord make you strong. Put on all the armour that God gives, so you can defend yourself against the devil's tricks.

EPHESIANS 6:10–11

293

Bible story link

In the last book of the Bible, there is a story about the archangel Michael fighting a dragon. It tells how the forces of good drove the devil from heaven. The dragon (representing the devil) and his angels were thrown down to earth, where he prowls around trying to trick human beings into his evil ways. (Story synopsis based on Revelation 12:7–9.)

The lift

I'm nine, and I've got lots of things to carry to school because I'm making cakes at after-school club tonight. I've got my cooking tin, my book bag, my lunch box and my trainers. My arms feel as if they're being stretched as I try to carry all those things.

We've got PE today. I don't like PE. We have to run round the playground three times before we start, and Jeremy Petrie always laughs at the way I run.

Today I'm walking to school on my own. I usually call for Julie but her mum phoned while I was eating my breakfast to say that Julie's been sick all night so she's not coming today.

A blue car is pulling up beside me. It's that lady who works at the corner shop where they sell cheese and cold meat. Mum bought some ham from her last Saturday. We ate it for tea with chips and a fried egg.

'Hello, Anjali,' she says. She has wound the window down and is smiling at me. 'You look as if you're struggling with all those bags. Do you want a lift? Your mum won't mind you getting in the car with me because we know each other, and it's going to rain soon.'

When I was very little—that's ages and ages ago—Mum told

me I was never to go with anyone unless they told me it was their birthday next week. Jan did that once. She lives next door to us. Mum was late home from work and asked Jan to pick me up from school without letting me know first. 'It's my birthday next week,' Jan said to me. Then I knew it was all right to go with her. But, as I say, that was ages ago and I don't need to bother with all that now.

The lady has got out of her car. She's wearing a white jumper and high-heeled shoes. She's opening the back door of the car and putting my bags on the seat. She is helping me to get in. Now she's closing the door and going back to the driver's seat.

'Are you going to work?' I ask her.

'Later,' she says, catching my eye in the mirror. Later. She is smiling in the mirror, at me, I think. I smile back. The car is turning left. It'll go right next, and then we're at school. It'll only take two minutes.

There's Sam. He's in my class at school. I wave at him. He nods back. He's carrying his cooking things, too.

'Don't wave,' the lady says. 'It's silly.'

She's driven past the end of the road where school is. She should have turned right. We're going towards the railway station now.

'You've missed the turn,' I say.

'I've got to fetch something from my house. You're early for school, what with me giving you a lift. What time do you have to be there?'

'Ten to nine,' I reply. She squints at her watch.

'Plenty of time,' she says.

I lift my hand and fiddle with the handle on the door. It doesn't move. She must have one of those child locks on, like Mum had when I was little. But suddenly a surge of energy rushes up to my face. I want to get out. I don't feel safe. I am trapped in a car with someone I don't really know, and I'm not quite sure where we're going.

Things children have said

'... you must always know who's picking you up...'

'... not all strangers want to hurt you. Some of them are kind, but you mustn't trust them...'

'... it's sad because when children get kidnapped you don't often hear that they have escaped... Anjali didn't know what was happening to her...'

'... you should never, ever, ever get in a car, even if you know the person, unless you've been told by someone you trust that it's OK...'

Thinking time for children

How can you keep yourself really safe? Think of a list of people you can completely trust. Why do you trust them?

Thinking time activity

Discuss all the possible endings to this story. Make a list of rules for keeping yourself really safe.

Prayer

Dear God, you know when someone is hurting or not feeling safe. Help us to keep ourselves as safe as possible all the time. Amen

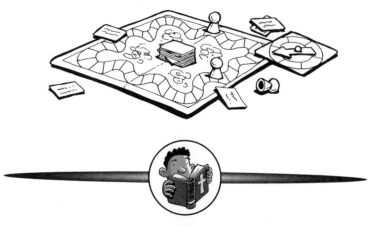

I don't like that

Story summary

Kerry's Uncle John plays games with her. She does not like playing with him. At school Kerry learns a poem that says she must say something if someone makes her feel unsafe. The story follows Kerry as she does just that, raising issues about when children might feel unsafe in someone else's company.

RE concept: Trusting others

 ## Exploring the concept

Children's understanding

- Talk about what it means to be safe with other people.
- Talk about who children can tell if they don't feel safe.

Religious overview

- Discuss who in a faith community could be trusted and why.

Christian viewpoint

Christians believe that anyone who causes harm to children in any way will have to answer to God for what he or she has done.

Do children agree with this viewpoint?

 ## Key Bible verses

'Don't be cruel to any of these little ones! I promise you that their angels are always with my Father in heaven.'

MATTHEW 18:10–11

 ## Bible story link

One day, some people brought their children to Jesus so that he could bless them. Jesus' disciples decided he was too busy. However, when they tried to turn the children away, Jesus insisted that they should not be stopped from coming to him. By putting the children first, he showed everyone how much he valued them. (Story synopsis based on Mark 10:13–14.)

Uncle John

'Uncle John's coming for supper tonight,' Mum said as Kerry opened the fridge door. The milk bottle froze in Kerry's hand and her tummy went all funny. There was something about Uncle John that she did not like.

'Can I have mine in the lounge on my own?' she asked.

'Kerry!' Mum sounded surprised. 'Uncle John comes to see you as well as me.'

Kerry knew that already. 'What time is he coming?' she asked.

'He said he'd drop in on the way home from work. You and I are his only family. You're very special to him. You know that, don't you?'

She knew that, too. He told her often enough. Kerry gave a half-nod. A funny feeling was rumbling round her body. It made her heart beat faster and her hands turn to jelly. It made her want to run—anywhere, just to get away from him. It made her feel sick.

She looked at Mum, peeling potatoes at the kitchen sink. 'How long is he staying?' she asked.

'I'm not sure, probably until about half past eight,' Mum said, without turning round. She did not see the look on Kerry's face.

'Does he have to come?' Kerry asked.

'Yes, he does,' Mum said. 'He's my brother and you are his niece and you behave yourself when he comes.'

'Oh,' Kerry said, thinking ahead. He would ask if he could read her a bedtime story. Upstairs. That was the bit she did not like.

Kerry finished drinking her milk and went to her bedroom. 'I'll find the shortest story I can,' she thought. 'He might not stay so long then.' She chose one with big writing and lots of pictures. It was a babyish story but that did not matter. It would only take five minutes to read.

Then she went downstairs and curled up in the big armchair. The television was on but all the time she was listening for the doorbell. Eventually it rang.

'John, how lovely to see you.' Mum's voice was welcoming.

'And you.' That was Uncle John's deep voice. 'And where's my favourite niece?'

He was in the lounge now, standing behind her. Kerry turned her face towards him and managed to smile.

'I've got a present for you,' he said, bending over to kiss her. Mum was standing by the door, smiling, watching. Kerry opened the bag. Inside was a game.

'Aren't you going to say "thank you"?' Mum said.

'Thank you,' Kerry whispered.

'Why don't the two of you come in the kitchen and work out how to play it while I finish getting supper ready?' Mum said.

'That's a good idea,' Uncle John smiled. 'Any chance of a cup of tea, too?'

Uncle John read the rules of the game out loud.

'Have you got that?' he asked, resting his arm on Kerry's shoulder. 'You be red and I'll be green.' His long fingers reached into the box and took out two plastic counters.

Mrs Harlow, her teacher, had once talked about 'oh-oh' feelings—those rumbling, jelly, sicky feelings you get when you don't feel safe. Mrs Harlow taught them a poem. They had written it out for handwriting practice.

> *If no one's ever there to see*
> *What happens to me secretly*
> *And I don't like what's going on*
> *I must be brave and tell someone.*
> *For if I don't, no one will know*
> *What it is that scares me so.*

Kerry suddenly knew what she had to do, but she did not feel brave, not like it said in the poem.

'I don't want to play this game any more,' she said.

'But Uncle John brought it specially for you.'

'I don't want to play it. I don't like playing games with Uncle John.'

Uncle John looked at Kerry. He wasn't smiling in the way he usually did.

'My little princess,' he gasped. 'You and I always play games together. What's the matter?'

'Kerry,' Mum gasped, 'that is so rude.'

Uncle John put his hand over the top of Kerry's. She snatched it away and stood up.

'I don't want to play,' she said again. Tears were pricking the backs of her eyes but she held on to them. 'I want to watch the television. On my own.'

Mum glared at her.

'You and I will talk about this later,' she said. She was angry, Kerry could tell. The poem hadn't said anyone would get angry with her. But it was too late now. She turned and left the room, taking her rumbling, jelly, sicky feelings with her.

When she reached the lounge, she curled up on the settee and buried her face in a cushion. She hated Uncle John. She hated the way he looked at her. She hated other things about him, too—things he said she must never talk about. But tonight she had stood up to him. Tonight she had been brave, but now there were muffled whispers in the hallway.

The front door opened and closed. Had Mum gone out and left her alone in the house with Uncle John?

Someone came into the lounge. Kerry did not dare look up to see who it was. Someone was sitting next to her. Only one person wore perfume like that, and that person loved her and would never want to hurt her.

'Mum,' she stammered. 'I don't like him.'

There was silence.

'He suddenly remembered he had to be somewhere else.' There was a puzzled tone to Mum's voice. 'Kerry, I want you to tell me exactly why you don't like Uncle John, and I want you to be completely honest.'

Things children have said

'... we think this story helps children understand that if someone was making them do things they didn't like, they must tell someone about it...'

'... someone I used to know made me feel funny...'

'... I don't like being with anyone who bullies me or other people...'

'... I wouldn't want to hurt their feelings, but I would tell someone about it...'

'... the worst thing would be if you trusted that person. Then you wouldn't know what to do and it would take longer to decide...'

'... I would say I had to go somewhere else and run away...'

'... I would try not to be rude to them...'

'... I would tell my mum and dad...'

'... I would tell my teacher...'

'... Kerry didn't like the way he played games with her...'

'... sometimes people have something odd about them. You must ask a grown-up you trust why. Then you will understand better. You might not want to see them again then...'

'... odd people are funny. I don't like being with them, especially if I'm on my own, so I make sure there's always someone else with me and we giggle about it afterwards...'

Thinking time for children

Is there anyone you don't like being with? Do you need to tell someone about it? Think of someone you could tell. When will you be seeing them next? Can you tell them then? Think what you will say to them.

Thinking time activity

Draw round your hand, and on the fingers and thumb write the names of five people you could tell if someone did something to you that made you unhappy.

Prayer

Dear God, sometimes I don't know what to do, especially if I'm really scared about something. Please help me to be brave and do the most sensible thing. Help me to find a grown-up I can trust. Amen

Bible index